D0843381

GRAPHIC DESIGN

The 50 most influential graphic designers in the world

First published in Great Britain in 2010

A & C Black Publishers Ltd
36 Soho Square
London W1D 3QY
www.acblack.com

ISBN: 978 1 4081 2002 6

Conceived and produced by
Elwin Street Limited
144 Liverpool Road
London N1 1LA
United Kingdom
www.elwinstreet.com

Design: James Lawrence
Advertising Archive: p.22; Alamy: pp. 11, 15, 16, 38, 58, 77; The Art Archive: pp. 55 (©
Seymour Chwast), 78, 97, 110, 117, 123; Corbis: pp. 9, 13, 21, 29, 36, 47, 61, 70, 83, 101
(© Hattula Moholy-Nagy/DACS 2009); Getty: pp. 45, 105; Mary Evans: p. 93; Pentagram:
p. 81 (designed by Angus Hyland); Rex Features: pp. 57, 74, 85; Takarazuka, Grand Revue,
1966, Courtesy of the Artist (Tadanori Yokoo): p. 35; Courtesy of the Artist (Ed Fella): p. 121;
Topfoto: pp. 7, 43, 65, 67, 73, 89, 99, 126; 2009. Museum of Modern Art, New York/Scala,
Florence: pp. 30 (© DACS 2009), 48, 53, 63 (© DACS 2009), 90, 106, 115.
Jacket picture credits: Front: The Art Archive; Back: Corbis.

Every effort was made to gain copyright clearances for the images used in this book.

A CIP catalogue record for this book is available from the British Library.

Printed in Singapore

PO_NUMBER: 14143

PO_STATUS: 1

Line Item No.: 2

QUANTITY: 1

Price Unit: $16.73

Price Line $CDN: $16.73

FUND_NAME: Creative Arts &Animat Bk

LOCATION_NAME: York General Collection

AUTHOR: GERBER, ANNA

TITLE_BRIEF:

GRAPHIC DESIGN : THE 50 MOST INFLUENTIAL GRAPHIC DESIGNERS IN THE WORLD.

ISBN: 140812002X

ISSN:

EDITION:

PUBLISHER: A & C BLACK LTD

SERIES: LITTLE BOOK OF BIG IDEAS.

BIB_ID: 311667

PUBLISHER_DATE: 2010

VENDOR_NAME: YBP Library Services

ES, AFD

12/12/2011 7:34:02 AM

REQUESTOR:

GRAPHIC DESIGN

The 50 most influential graphic designers in the world

ANNA GERBER

CONTENTS

Commercial art, Branding, Signs and Symbols

Typefaces and Typography

INTRODUCTION

There can be no doubt that graphic design has long played an important, influential role in everyday life. One only needs to consider the role of Russian constructivists in their use of visual tools to promote post-revolution Soviet state propaganda to observe this. Take a look at the unconventional impact of the Italian futurist movement on book design or consider how American corporate identity design has influenced the reputations, brands and fortunes of countless globally renowned corporations, and the same is true.

From the earliest developments in graphic design – the invention of the Linotype hot-metal line-casting machine in 1886, for example – all the way to the intentionally illegible anarchy that epitomised David Carson's art direction of *Ray Gun* magazine over 100 years later, the events chronicled in this book, viewed as a whole, offer a fascinating, if sometimes bumpy and circuitous mosaic of the journey undertaken by graphic design as a profession from 1850 to the present day. Highlights on this progress include the pioneering design principles laid down by the Bauhaus design school in 1930s' Germany, Alexei Brodovitch's defining stint as art director of *Harper's Bazaar* magazine in New York in the 1950s and American designer April Greiman's pioneering incorporation of computer technology into her graphic design practice during the 1980s.

The most influential design styles and trends are discussed alongside explanations as to how and why they came about and what they involved. Subjects covered include Aleksander Rodchenko's

'We will employ everything it takes to make a busy passer-by stop in his tracks.'

Vladimir Stenberg

experiments with photomontage in book design; the explosive optical, psychedelic poster designs of Tadanori Yokoo; Gustav Klutsis's visually powerful state-sponsored Soviet propaganda pieces; the dependence of the Swiss Style typographers on just one typeface – Akzidenz Grotesk – for their most influential work; and how Hermann Zapf's Verdana came to be the generic typeface within all of Microsoft's operating systems.

Considering the unique accomplishments of 50 designers and their studios, the book is organised by theme – Poster Design; Books and Magazines; Commercial Art, Branding, Signs and Symbols; and Typefaces and Typography. Covering the major stylistic movements to influence graphic design, including art nouveau, futurism, modernism, constructivism and Dadaism, as well as the major developmental milestones (lithography, Monotype, digitised fonts), each fascinating story is presented in clear and accessible, yet historically rigorous and accurate terms. The result is a substantive, multi-perspective overview of the lives and achievements of those practitioners who did much to push various aspects of graphic design to new, boundary-breaking pastures.

Jules Cheret

Until the late nineteenth century the advertising poster was created primarily by craftsmen working in printing shops. It most commonly featured simple, gridded letterpress typography with occasional rudimentary woodblock or etched images. Influenced by the colourful pictures and riotous subject matter of American circus posters, Frenchman Jules Cheret enlivened the poster as a medium by adding colour, movement and a heretofore-unseen sense of pictorial sophistication. In doing so, he magnificently captured the spirit of the French Belle Epoque.

Born 1836, Paris, France
Importance
Revolutionised and
modernised the
advertising poster
Died 1932, Nice, France

In 1881 an influential law to help promote free speech was passed in France, which allowed the use of posters on all buildings other than schools, places of worship and public entities. Originally invented in Austria in 1796, the advertising poster became prolific in French cities in the wake of this law, with French printers dominating the business and perfecting the art of lithography. At the same time, Paris became a cultural capital with a booming consumer society and a leisure class who enjoyed nightclubs, cabarets and restaurants. Cheret demonstrated a natural ability to capture and illustrate the excitement and appeal of these entertainment establishments in poster form – an ability that was much valued by their owners.

The son of a typesetter and apprenticed to a lithographer since 1849, Cheret was also instrumental in developing a revolutionary system for producing four-colour lithography by using a guide or 'keyline'. He drew on the printing stone itself, allowing for a fluidity of line and bringing immediacy to the process. It was also possible to make subtle changes quickly. Like many of his art nouveau colleagues

(Henri de Toulouse-Lautrec, Alphonse Mucha, Theophile-Alexandre Steinlen), Cheret was also greatly influenced by the traditional Japanese woodblock prints or *ukiyo-e*, popular collectables at the time. He admired their expressive contour, use of simple flat areas of colour, the rhythmic quality of line and the frequent absence of a central perspective. In his 1879 poster for L'Horloge, a cabaret on the Champs Elysée, the figures danced in an undefined space, appearing to float. Their elongated limbs were exaggerated and their simple two-dimensionality suggested an interest in abstraction reminiscent of the *ukiyo-e*. Rarely did Cheret's works contain a true narrative; instead they frequently featured an elegant, well-dressed woman enjoying a pastime (such as skating or eating). So prevalent was this in his work that these women became known as 'Cherettes'.

Cheret's 1896 poster featuring the fashionable Palais de Glace, one of his most admired works.

During his long career Cheret designed over 1,000 posters. Perhaps the best example of his mature work is the 1893 poster for a performance by Loïe Fuller at the Folies Bergère. The spinning Fuller – a major star of the day – with her bright red hair and shining dress, performs a dance in a semi-transparent and diaphanous gown. The poster is a tour de force, capturing both the energy of her performance and its eroticism. It is no wonder that Cheret's contemporary, French writer Félix Fénéon, wrote of the poster, 'Look at the art of the street. There instead of pictures in gold frames you will find real-life art, coloured posters.'

Alphonse Mucha

Alphonse Mucha epitomised the style now familiarly known as French art nouveau. In doing so he helped to raise the level of sophistication for the visual, as well as the narrative, quality of a poster. His colourful, elaborate and decorative designs have become the most imitated and archetypal of this period.

Born 1860, Ivančice, Moravia (now Czech Republic)
Importance Brilliantly interpreted the French art nouveau style.
Died 1939, Prague, Moravia (now Czech Republic)

Characteristically, the art nouveau movement was an attempt to unite the functional arts of architecture, design and graphics in an entirely new anti-historical and original style. Its signifying stylistic feature was the use of excessive ornament and decoration whose genesis lay in nature. Central to the movement was a reaction to the implications of the industrial revolution. As such, its designers embraced the curving, seemingly random and slightly threatening lines produced in untamed nature. Such motifs, alongside the depiction of willowy female figures, were characteristic of the movement and Mucha was a master of this type of representation.

Born in Moravia (now the Czech Republic), Mucha had left his homeland to pursue painting opportunities in Vienna and Munich, and he eventually settled in Paris. The influence of his birthplace never really dissipated, however. In a poster for Job cigarette papers, Mucha sat the female figure in an undefined space surrounded by Arab-style tiles. Moravian folk art often featured in his work, as seen in the staff held by the willowy figure in his 1896 poster for the Salon de Cent. One of his first, and most important, clients was the actress Sarah Bernhardt, portrayed by Mucha as the heroic Hamlet slaying a mythical dragon. Such forced exoticism reflected Mucha's own interest in magic and the occult. Unlike the females who occupy the works of the other French artists at the time – Cheret and Toulouse-Lautrec, for example – Mucha's are mysterious, ethereal and not particularly welcoming. They have no easily recognisable nationality or ethnicity; instead they suggest something foreign and forbidding. Often they seem to be in a state of intoxication or dreamlike pensiveness.

Like many of his contemporaries, Mucha was enthralled by the Japanese traditional woodblock print or *ukiyo-e* – which, along with the art nouveau poster, was often collected and displayed as a work of art as well as being used as a commercial entity for advertisements – and his work betrays their influence. Above all, however, his posters reflect his training as a painter, particularly in their extravagance of colour and detail in drawing, which were unlike anything seen before and created significant new possibilities in terms of subject matter and formal style for all future graphic designers.

Mucha's poster Bières de la Meuse (1898) expresses his interest in the sensual and stylised female form.

The Beggarstaff Brothers

Although the Beggarstaff Brothers produced just 12 finished poster designs, their work proved enormously influential on later generations and marked a radical departure from the decorative designs of the art nouveau, Vienna Secession and Jugendstil movements that had dominated late-nineteenth-century design.

Born (James Pryde) 1866, Edinburgh, Scotland; (William Nicholson) 1872, Newark, England
Importance The first designers to demonstrate a modernist attraction to functionalism
Died (James Pryde) 1941, London, England; (William Nicholson) 1949, London, England

While the French were obsessed with the depiction of elegant, elongated women and uncontrolled nature, in England there were radical works being produced at the opposite end of the spectrum, in a series of remarkable posters designed and created by the Beggarstaff Brothers (James Pryde and William Nicholson). As brothers-in-law, Pryde and Nicholson completely dismissed the elaborate surface decoration of the art nouveau, Englishmen Aubrey Beardsley and William Morris and the Vienna Secession. They presented a tremendously simplified illustrative world that was extraordinarily prescient of many of the minimalist experiments that occurred in Germany almost 30 years later (see New Typography, page 108). Remarkably, the Beggarstaffs' reductivist images were created during just five years of collaboration, from 1894 to 1899.

Both Pryde and Nicholson were trained as painters and had decided to start a commercial poster company under a pseudonym, the Beggarstaff Brothers, which suggested something solid and definitively English. In fact, the name simply came from a brand of animal fodder. Their desire to create commercial design was influenced by the artist/socialist William Morris, who called for the accessibility of beautiful things for all. Although influenced by Morris's politics, writings and lectures, the Beggarstaffs took a completely opposite approach stylistically, rejecting his natural ornate and reactionary style in favour of far simpler forms, notably of the human figure. Many of their works cleverly play with negative and positive space and the empty white of the page. Figures frequently stand alone in empty spaces, isolated and without any clear narrative.

In order to save money, Pryde and Nicholson used inexpensive papers and a relatively primitive stencil to produce their works, which they then coloured by hand. They used a limited colour palette commonly featuring red, yellow and orange, which they believed visually cut through the rain and fog so common in England at the time. Even their sans-serif type, cut out from the stencil, suggested a strong desire for clarity.

Perhaps their masterpiece is an austere poster for a production of *Hamlet* from 1894. The lonely prince and the poster's severe minimalism echo the inherent melancholy of Shakespeare's play. However, their designs often proved too problematic visually and narratively for their clients. A Rowntree's Cocoa poster (1895), with three non-interactive figures floating above each other, even inspired a contest by the manufacturer to help determine its meaning.

Although these works must have seemed extraordinary in their day, they suggest an early modernist attraction to functionalism and sparseness and a concern for readability in the context of a busy street.

This theatre poster showcases the Beggarstaffs' limited yet effective palette.

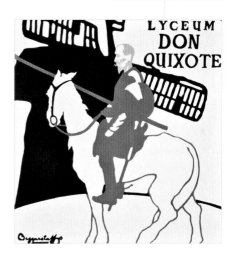

Ludwig Hohlwein

Ludwig Hohlwein produced some of the most successful and popular posters printed in Germany between the two great wars. Sensitive to the whims of the German bourgeoisie, Holhwein's work was remarkably innovative in its adaptation of pictorial convention. His work proved so popular and accessible that Adolf Hitler, during the mid-thirties, chose Hohlwein to be the Nazi party's primary poster designer.

Born 1874, Wiesbaden, Germany
Importance Excelled in designing posters that appealed to the middle-class consumer
Died 1949, Berchtesgarten, Germany

Trained as an architect, Hohlwein turned to graphic design in 1906 and at the height of his fame and success he led a large and important office. Unlike Lucian Bernhard, who predicted and embraced the coming transformation in design that was to culminate in the modernist movement, New Typography and Russian constructivism (see pages 108 and 40), Hohlwein derived inspiration from a desire to portray the status quo: the ruddy-cheeked, affluent bourgeoisie of his native Munich. Although he was influenced by the Beggarstaff Brothers, Hohlwein was never able to forgo narrative in his posters and they seem timid by contrast. They remain straightforwardly descriptive, featuring upper-middle-class women riding horses and men sporting new clothes.

Hohlwein's work was painterly in spirit. In the manner in which an architect works, some of his images were achieved through a build up of unrelated shapes. Hints of cubist collage and even surrealism are present; flattened figures play off three-dimensional forms side by side. By using photographs of figures taken in very bright sunlight, he emphasised the highlights and enhanced the legibility of his posters.

Many of his early posters for clothing outlets, such as Hermann Scherrer, suggest a connection to the formal experiments of both

Pablo Picasso and Georges Braque. In the poster for Scherrer's riding clothes, Hohlwein seemed to attach a piece of fabric – using illustration – as if to form an actual collage. This clever technique exaggerated the tailoring role of the shops and also reaffirmed the artificiality of the poster medium. In other works, such as the powerful poster for Pelican inks featuring just ink-coloured handprints, Hohlwein showed an openness to new ideas and a willingness to employ abstraction.

Perhaps most alarming in Hohlwein's career was the overall shift in the character of work that began in the early 1930s, and which paralleled the political changes and the rise of fascism taking place in Germany at the time. Some of his work began to take on a darkness and a certain unrestrained military machismo, as seen in the war propaganda poster *Und du?* of 1929 in which a menacing shadow-faced German soldier asks 'And you?'; in other words, what are you contributing to the war effort? Other works, including a poster for the 1936 Winter Olympics, are saccharin and disturbing in their depiction of the heroic German, and portray an almost Aryan stereotype of the German middle class – blonde and sturdy.

AUSKÜNFTE UND WERBESCHRIFTEN DURCH ALLE REISE- UND VERKEHRSBÜROS DES IN-UND AUSLANDES

Hohlwein's narrative-based posters idealised the German bourgeoisie.

It is hard to separate Hohlwein from this dark period in history, as he took an official role in producing propaganda for the Nazi Party. Not surprisingly, after the war there was little work for Hohlwein in Germany, impoverished and defeated, and he died soon after, in 1949.

Lucian Bernhard

German designer Lucian Bernhard continued many of the reductivist experiments that the Beggarstaff Brothers and Peter Behrens had initiated. As such, his typography, logos and posters – with their inherent emphasis on clarity – directly foreshadowed the remarkable revolution in the graphic arts that took place in Germany and much of the rest of western Europe between the First and Second World Wars.

Born 1883, Stuttgart, Germany
Importance Pre-empted the modernist fascination with new technology
Died 1972, New York City, New York, United States

Working in Berlin from 1905 to 1923, Bernhard became a designer somewhat by chance when a design he composed for Preistler matches won a competition sponsored by the owner of one of Germany's largest printers, Hollerbaum & Schmidt. By eliminating much

A 1914 Sachsplatz *for coffee brings the product to the forefront of the poster.*

of the decorative excess of the art nouveau and the Vienna Secession, and by limiting himself to the straightforward illustration of just the product and its brand name, Bernhard produced some of the world's very first *Sachplakats* or 'object posters'.

Sometimes known as 'factual posters', these were an important departure for the medium, allowing the designer to do away with any exaggerated claims, scantily clad women or even a basic story line – elements that had been standard up until this time (and are still common in much poster design today). These factual posters continued to be popular throughout the twentieth century, particularly in Switzerland, where the candour and perceived honesty of this kind of advertisement was greatly valued.

Importantly, Bernhard's work predicted the modernist fascination with and appreciation of new technology and the machine (particularly in Germany). His simple posters for Osram light bulbs and Bosch auto parts extolled a new-found beauty in simple industrial objects, raising them above the stature of the ordinary and, ultimately, celebrating the possibilities of science and technology.

ATF
The American Type Founders company (ATF) was the name given to 23 US foundries who merged in 1892 in order to compete with the emergence of new typesetting machines, the Linotype and Monotype (see also page 18).

Masterful as a draughtsman and innovative in the colour palette he used, Bernhard also designed many of the accompanying logos for the brands. His beautifully-illustrated Bosch sparkplug poster seemed to explode like some sort of cartoon and has been considered prescient of much 1960s pop art.

In 1923, Bernhard emigrated to America, seeking better employment opportunities, leaving his family and wife in Berlin. Although he met with much success working for corporations such as Amoco, Pepsi and Ex-lax, and designing numerous typefaces for the American Type Founders (ATF) – including the very popular Bernhard Gothic – his American poster designs were never fully accepted.

LINOTYPE AND MONOTYPE

The mechanisation of typesetting in the United States in the late 1880s proved hugely transformative for both graphic design and graphic designers. The technology meant the slow fading out of hand-set typography and, in its place, industrial speed turnaround and heightened quality in all detail.

The first machine to enable this process was called the Linotype, invented in 1886. It was invented by Ottmar Mergenthaler as a hot-metal line-casting machine, known informally as the 'blower'. Quickly, it was renamed the Linotype, a compression of what it did – easily render a line of type, set and justified. The Linotype was prototyped and put to use by the Mergenthaler Linotype Company, based in Brooklyn.

According to Phil Baines's and Andrew Haslam's book *Type & Typography*, the Linotype 'combined keyboard unit, matrix magazine and caster in one machine. Matrices were assembled in line as a result of the operation of the keyboard and when each line was complete, the machine cast it as a single piece of metal (usually called a slug).'

Speaking more generally in his book *Graphic Design: A New History*, Stephen J Eskilson summarises the mechanical breakthrough of the Linotype as follows: '(It) allowed typsetters to work with a

> *'A number of abortive attempts were made to mechanize the composition of type... The answer was found in the shape of machines which both cast and composed type.'*
>
> Jonathan Rose

punch keyboard that directly controlled machinery for casting hot metal type.'

The Linotype was followed by the rival Monotype machine, invented by Tolbert Lanston, who took out a patent for his creation in 1887. His Monotype composing machine was prototyped and manufactured by the Lanston Monotype Machine Company, founded in Washington DC in 1887. It differed from the Linotype, in that it offered typesetters a system of compiling letters one by one (hence Monotype), the advantage of this being that it was easier to isolate any corrections that needed to be made. It also enabled kerning – the adjustment of spacing between individual characters – an option that was not available with the Linotype.

The precise mechanics of this process are described as follows in *Type & Typography*: 'The operation of the keyboard resulted in two holes being punched in a paper ribbon: these were the coordinates of the character in the matrix case waiting in the casting unit. Once the keyboarding was complete, the ribbon was taken to the caster. As the ribbon was fed through, the matrix moved into position and type was cast letter by letter.'

The competition to become market leader instigated price wars and fierce strategy battles between Linotype and Monotype as each company strived to establish an advantage over its rival. The Linotype machine was introduced to the British market when Mergenthaler Linotype & Machinery Ltd opened in Manchester. At the same time, Monotype systems were installed at leading British printers, such as Butler & Tanner, in Frome, Somerset.

The boom continued until the 1950s, when offset lithographic printing and photosetting systems came onto the market and became more popular. This led to the slow decline of metal typesetting and letterpress printing. By 1970, Linotype ceased producing its line-casting machine; Monotype continued to be produced until 1987.

Edward McKnight Kauffer

Although born in the United States, Edward McKnight Kauffer went on to become the most important and prolific English poster designer of the period between the two world wars. Kauffer helped to transform what had been the relatively primitive English poster into a sophisticated art form.

Born 1890, Great Falls, Montana, United States
Importance United poster design with the fine arts
Died 1954, New York City, New York, United States

Kauffer came to England in 1914 following a tour of the Continent and became stranded there after the outbreak of the First World War. Born simply Edward Kauffer, he had adopted his middle name, McKnight, in honour of an influential art professor with whom he had studied in the United States and who had sponsored his trip to Europe.

Throughout his career, Kauffer's work was exclusively painterly and illustrative in nature and stressed aesthetics over clear or straightforward communication. His posters often functioned as a kind of sophisticated urban decoration for the streets and subways on which they were posted. Kauffer's largest, and by far his most productive, client was the London Underground under the direction of astute publicity manager, Frank Pick. Many of his works for the company promoted the underground itself, such as the art-deco-inspired *Power, the Nerve Centre of London's Underground* (1931), while others, such as *Shop Between 10 and 4* (1930) encouraged a particular kind of use of the trains. Some of Kauffer's most charming posters promote train travel to small rural English towns. In many of these, such as a 1930 poster advertising travel to Uxbridge, he used a simplified number of colours and simple flat areas of ink, reminiscent of the type of work produced by earlier English poster designers, the Beggarstaff Brothers.

A number of Kauffer's posters referenced, adapted and borrowed from many of the avant-garde fine art movements of the day, including futurism, cubism, surrealism and the art deco movement. In each case Kauffer borrowed small amounts of visual vocabulary and adapted them to his otherwise realistic works. A well-known example of this is his use of cubist-style shapes to represent flying birds in his famous 1918 poster for the *Daily Herald* newspaper.

Significantly, Pick and Kauffer did not just see posters as a means of advertising a product; instead they pioneered the concept of the poster as a way of promoting public art education and beautifying the urban environment. Frequently copies of the posters were also available for sale to the public. In 1937 Edward McKnight Kauffer became the first poster designer to have a retrospective exhibition at New York's Museum of Modern Art (MoMA). He moved to New York in 1941 and continued to work for a variety of clients including, the American Red Cross, American Airlines and publishers Alfred Knopf and Random House.

Kauffer's airline posters, such as this 1948 example, combine great charm with a strong aesthetic sense of the poster as public art.

The Ideologist
Gustav Klutsis

Avant-garde Russian graphic designer and poster designer Gustav Klutsis was best known for his constructivist political photomontage works, many of which served to promote Soviet and Stalinist propaganda.

Born 1895, Koni, Latvia
Importance
Championed art as a means of spreading a political message
Died 1938, Moscow, Russia

Born in 1895, Gustav Klutsis was drafted into the Russian army in 1915 and helped overthrow Tsar Nicholas II in 1917. Discharged a year later, he became a card-carrying member of the communist party. In 1919, he studied art in Kazimir Malevic's studio and began to experiment with constructivist-influenced politically-infused photomontage for posters such as *Dynamic City* and *Lenin and Electrification*, each of which supported Soviet state ideology.

In 1920 Klutsis began teaching colour theory at Vkhutemas, the state-sponsored art and design school. It was here that he met and married the art student Valentina Kulagina, with whom he would collaborate for the rest of his life. Under Stalinism, Klutsis used illustration, photography, sculpture and mostly photomontage (often referred to in his particular case as political photomontage) to celebrate the values and ideals of the communist state.

One of Klutsis's most famous works, Under the Banner of Lenin *(1930) overlays Lenin's face with that of Stalin.*

A member of the constructivist movement, along with Aleksander Rodchenko, Klutsis used the photomontage approach in his 1928 poster, *Spartakiada Moscow*, advertising the athletic games in Moscow. Using an eclectic combination of half-tone photographs, gelatin silver prints and coloured paper, Klutsis collaged a diverse selection of photographs (for example: a female athlete standing, smiling, with her hands behind her back; two sets of boxers sparring; a weightlifter crouching and holding a giant weight aloft with only one hand; two men wrestling) with assorted, rough-hewn lettering cut from what appeared to be industrial construction paper. The result was a poster bristling with energy, encapsulating the physicality and unpredictability of the athletic bouts and competitions at the Moscow games.

In 1930, a typical poster for the state publishing house promoting socialist construction, titled *Under The Banner of Lenin*, laid photographs of Lenin and Stalin upon one another, creating an ideological montage commentary. Klutsis remarked on the necessity of methods such as photomontage, to support the political message, emphasising the need for the role of art within society: 'The old disciplines in the visual arts (drawing, painting, graphic art), with obsolete techniques and working methods, are insufficient to satisfy the demands of the Revolution as concerns the tasks of agitation and propaganda on a massive scale – art must be on the same high level as socialist industry.'

Despite Klutsis and his wife's joint dedicated political loyalty and artistic support of Stalin and the state (his wife worked for the State Art Publishing Agency, Izogiz), Klutsis was arrested in Moscow in January 1938, on the eve of his departure to the World's Fair in New York. Kulagina was told that he had been imprisoned at the Butovo prison, and later that he had died of a heart attack in 1944. Only in 1989 was it revealed that on Stalin's order, Klutsis had been executed. It is still unclear why this was the case, given his lifelong affinity to the Party, though some believe that he was accused of having been a traitor. Klutsis's work is today regarded as a leading example of the constructivist style, primarily owing to his bold and celebrated experiments with photomontage.

POLITICS & PROPAGANDA

Although the poster became a popular means of selling during the second half of the nineteenth century, following the advent of the lithographic printing process, it wasn't until the outbreak of the First World War that it assumed its role as a socially-charged tool of mass communication.

B efore the First World War broke out, the poster as a popular art form had been characterised predominantly by the art nouveau style that had prevailed since the end of the nineteenth century. Now, with the onset of war, posters assumed a new role as visual media and a means of propaganda, offering the ideal opportunity for governments to communicate on a mass scale. Posters became conduits for political messages, public morale boosting and the recruitment of armed forces. The most iconic and widely imitated poster of this era appeared across Britain in 1914, designed by Alfred Leete. It featured an illustrated portrait of Lord Kitchener, the then Secretary of State for War, pointing his finger out at a nameless everyman, with the message: 'Britons, Lord Kitchener Wants You. Join Your Country's Army! God Save the King'. The poster was designed to entice Britons to enlist, since conscription to the armed forces was not yet active.

In Russia as well, the role of the poster as propaganda played a significant role in everyday Soviet life following the Revolution of 1917. State propaganda was promoted across the Soviet Union using bold poster designs, which had to be visually powerful (as opposed to being text led), since many of those in the targeted communities were illiterate. Early post-revolution posters tended to assume a classical power as, demonstrated by Nikolay Kochergin's *Long Live The Red Army* (1920), which featured a rousing illustration of the Red Army in the throes of battle. Many of the posters generated around this time were designed by artists operating under the umbrella of Russian constructivism (see page 40), who espoused what was called productivism – the creation of artworks expressly supportive of the goals of the communist state.

The constructivists' pioneering employment of photomontage (see page 68), featured prominently in their state-sponsored mass-produced poster designs and led to a strong, distinctive visual language that, today, is inseparable from historical depictions of Soviet propaganda. The poster designs of Gustav Klutsis, an official state poster designer, typify the posters generated during this era. One such poster by Klutsis, the socialist-realist photomontaged *Civilised Life – Productive Work* (1932), featured a photograph of a proud, strong worker, protective goggles on forehead, standing before an idealised modern landscape. The slogan was stamped over both halves of the image, the whole designed to sell the propaganda of Stalin's first Five Year Plan to members of the Communist Youth Organisation.

The use of posters featured heavily in the Nazi regime's promotion of party and government ideology in the years that preceded the Second World War. Josef Goebbels oversaw the Ministry of Propaganda and National Enlightenment, and his policy-making ensured that Germany experienced the mass-media branding of the National Socialist message. With Hitler in power, graphic design was subject to the same strict clampdown as other media, and designers were ordered to abandon all international modernist styles of the era and to focus on the glorification of the Nazi machine instead. Nazi propaganda posters were rife with the reappropriated symbol of the swastika, images of perceived German national strength and might, references glorifying the 'führer', and incessant anti-Semitism.

Since the end of the Second World War, the poster, despite the advent of the power of television and later technological developments facilitating mass communication, has continued to play a significant role in communicating politics.

The Stenberg Brothers

The Stenberg brothers, Vladimir and Georgii, were at the forefront of the radical contructivist movement that gained momentum in Russia in the late 1920s. Shunning the bourgeois connotations of the fine artist, they embraced the term 'constructor' rather than 'designer', which suggested that they constructed or built things much like an engineer or architect does. Among the work they created in this highly distinctive style were the most successful and important film poster designs of the period.

Born (Vladimir) 1899, Moscow, Russia; (Georgii) 1900, Moscow, Russia
Importance Revolutionised the art of the film poster
Died (Vladimir) 1982, Moscow, Russia; (Georgii) 1933, Moscow, Russia

Even more momentous than the developments taking place in the rest of Europe in the 1920s were those that accompanied the Bolshevik Revolution of 1917 in Russia. In overthrowing the monarchy and establishing a communist state, the Bolsheviks hoped to create an entirely new social structure that included a new economic and political system. They believed that in this new society a revolution in the arts was also necessary – one that made the arts more beholden to the well-being of the populace and, ultimately, to the state's needs for self-aggrandizing propaganda. Lenin loved film and the communists understood that while film was an excellent way in which to entertain the masses, it could also be a wonderful conduit of information. Alongside the raised status of film and theatre came a uniquely important place in society for graphic design: all three became ideal tools for spreading the new Bolshevik state's propaganda.

Responsible for the first published statement underlying the principles of constructivism, the Stenberg brothers concluded the piece with, 'After weighing the facts on the scales of an honest attitude to earth's inhabitants, the constructivists declare art and its priests illegal.' They worked in a unique way and created their vibrant illustrated work with the use of a sophisticated projection device that allowed them to draw images in the manner of photomontage (see page 68). This afforded a flexibility that was impossible to achieve with simple black and white photographs. In their poster for the *Eleventh*, for example, the distorted perspective of the face was only conceivable through the use of this imaging machine. Other works like *Symphony of a Great City* (1928), showed the brothers' innate ability to borrow from disparate sources.

The sophistication of the posters designed by the Stenberg brothers owes much to the influence of Russian cinema at the time. The great Russian director Sergei Eisenstein said of film that it was a series of 'collisions', and much of this is true for the Stenbergs' graphic work. They introduced a completely new sense of movement, elapsed time and even utilised the extreme close-up – all of which were quite new to film advertisements. Instead of portraying the film's star in one particular scene (a technique still common today), the brothers tried to express the atmosphere of the film and often evoked the humour, melancholy or sexiness of the work. The close to three hundred works produced by them remain some of the most visually sophisticated film posters ever produced in the history of the medium.

The Punch: *a typically innovative, photomontage-like film poster.*

A M Cassandre

During the peak of his career, in the 1930s, A M Cassandre revolutionised the art of poster design, taking it from a relatively 'primitive' device to new heights of sophistication, both visually and in terms of narrative. His work introduced a level of psychological complexity and manipulation of the viewer that had never been seen before in the medium.

Born 1901, Kharkov, Ukraine
Importance The most famous and most prolific poster designer of all time
Died 1968, Paris, France

Having mastered the art of the lithographic process in the late nineteenth century, and thus invented the modern poster, the French continued to use the lithograph as a major vehicle for advertising up until, and even after, the Second World War. It was during this time that Cassandre became the most successful of the second generation of poster designers that followed the innovations of Henri de Toulouse-Lautrec, Jules Cheret and Alphonse Mucha.

Born Adolphe Mouron in the Ukraine in 1901, Cassandre moved to Paris during the First World War and studied painting at the Ecole des Beaux Arts. Immediately upon arriving in Paris he was immersed in the avant-garde fine art movements that included the revolutionary work of the cubists, surrealists and the purists. His painterly poster style borrowed heavily from these influences as well as the contemporary art deco movement. He frequently mimicked the coloration of the cubists' work – primarily earth tones – as well as the shading technique called

'Today's man… admires brevity, the straight line, prefers violence over force… That is why he loves the poster and why for him it is his most authentic expression.'

'cubist umbre'. From the surrealists he borrowed many of the visual tricks that gave his work its immediate impact and, like the purists, he often used simplified geometric shapes.

In 1923, Cassandre began work for an important lithographic printer, Hatchard et Compagnie, and soon after changed his name, choosing the pseudonym Cassandre after the clairvoyant daughter of the King of Troy from Homer's *Illiad*. In 1927 he and Charles Loupot co-founded the Alliance Graphique Internationale, beginning his most prolific period during which he worked for a wide range of clients including the French National Railroad, Ford Motor Company and numerous spirit companies and restaurants.

Throughout the 1930s, Cassandre produced iconic advertisements that covered many of the walls along Paris streets. In addition to posters, he designed a

Cassandre believed posters were a strong instrument for communication.

number of typefaces during this period, including his most important – Peignot. He also worked for art director Alexei Brodovitch at *Harper's Bazaar*, designing covers, and became interested in costume and set design.

After the Second World War, Cassandre's style remained primarily painterly; without the use of photography it appeared old-fashioned and commissions soon declined. However, he continued to occupy himself with set design and some graphic work, including his iconic logo for the French designer Yves Saint Laurent (1963).

Josef Müller-Brockmann

Josef Müller-Brockmann came to prominence in the 1950s and has since become best known as a pioneer of the Swiss Style: a post-constructivist approach to design that relied heavily on a strong text–image relationship, and that was regulated by the use of the 'grid' – a system used by graphic designers to assist with structuring the content of a page.

Born 1914, Rappersil, Switzerland
Importance Championed the Swiss Style, renowned for its use of the grid
Died 1996, Zurich, Switzerland

The Swiss Style emerged in the 1950s, rising out of the International Style that had been taking shape in neighbouring countries from the 1920s onwards. The unique style saw designers like Müller-Brockman using exclusively sans-serif typefaces (and later, just one typeface – Akzidenz Grotesk), bold photographs as opposed to illustrations and minimalist composition dictated by the grid. Today, historians look to a series of posters designed by Müller-Brockmann for Zurich town hall promoting concert performances as being most emblematic of the Swiss Style.

Müller-Brockmann studied architecture, design and history of art in Zurich, before working as a freelance graphic designer and illustrator. He opened his own design studio in 1936. After serving in the Second World War,

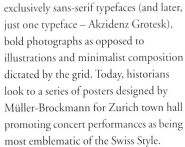

An anti-noise pollution poster from 1960 in typical Swiss Style, with sans-serif photography.

he once more worked as a graphic designer, specialising in exhibition design and illustration. At the start of the 1950s, he began to move towards what is now known as an objective-constructive design approach. This assumed a clear identity in 1951, when Müller-Brockmann became a member of Alliance Graphique Internationale.

The earliest indications of the emerging Swiss Style appeared in Müller-Brockmann's 1953 road-safety poster for the Swiss Automobile Club, titled *Mind That Child!*, a black-and-white, close-cropped photograph of a car hurtling towards a running child. The design altered the scale of the images for added effect (the car is disproportionately larger than the child) and used bold white type. This was the start of a near-exclusive use of Akzidenz Grotesk, a sans-serif typeface that is now seen as a precursor to Helvetica, and which took its inspiration from the work of earlier German trade printers.

THE ALLIANCE GRAPHIQUE INTERNATIONALE Formed in Paris in 1951, this is a by-invitation-only professional club, for the world's most distinguished graphic designers and artists.

In 1958, Müller-Brockmann, along with Richard P Lohse, Hans Neuburg and Carlo Vivarelli, launched the magazine *Neue Grafik* (*New Graphic Design*), which featured the work of Swiss designers while contemplating the state of 'modern graphic and applied art'. The magazine, whose editors were influenced by Russian constructivism (see page 40), later tagged Müller-Brockman's seminal Zurich concert posters as examples of *konstruktive Grafik*.

As such bold new visions of graphic design attracted international attention, Müller-Brockmann's studio expanded and became the epicentre of the Swiss Style. *Neue Grafik*, in tandem with Müller-Brockmann's lecturing position at the Zurich School of Arts and Crafts and the founding of Müller-Brockmann & Co advertising agency in 1967, solidified his growing reputation as designer, critic and educator.

Müller-Brockmann also contributed to the graphic design discourse through the publication of several notable books, namely *The Graphic Artist and his Design Problems* (1961), *A History of Visual Communication* and *A History of the Poster* (both 1971) and *A Grid System for Graphic Designers* (1981).

SWISS STYLE

The Swiss Style of design emerged in Switzerland following the Second World War. Once it had succeeded in popularising its distinctive approach to graphic design across Europe, Swiss Style – also referred to as International Style – moved on to the United States, where it triggered an unprecedented boom in US corporate identity design.

Emerging in the early 1950s, the Swiss Style was a graphic design movement that promoted legibility, objectivity and clean, simple design. Key elements of the style included sans-serif typefaces, asymmetrical layouts, an adherence to a grid system for page layouts and a tendency towards ranged-left, ragged-right text placement. The leading figures of the style, Josef Müller-Brockmann and Karl Gerstner, favoured the incorporation of photographic images in their designs, revealing the influence of the Bauhaus 'typo-foto' and Russian constructivism in their approach (see pages 102 and 40).

The roots of Swiss Style design hark back to the 1930s, when a group of Swiss designers were vigorously receptive to the influence of the New Typography that had been pioneered by Jan Tschichold, among others, at the Bauhaus. Artists like Max Bill studied at the Bauhaus school and returned to Switzerland demonstrating what they had learned with Bauhaus-influenced posters, such as Bill's *Prehistorical Rock Paintings of South Africa* (1931). In 1933, when the Bauhaus school was closed by the Nazis, Tschichold went into exile in Basel, where he worked mostly as a book designer. At the same time, Anton Stankowski, known for his 'industrial graphics', settled in Zurich (also in exile), where he created advertisements that were typically designed in the sans-serif typeface Akzidenz Grotesk, laid out asymetrically and making use of rules. All of this came together with the founding of the Basel School of Design (Schule für Gestaltung

Basel) in 1947 by Emil Ruder, author of a book on typography that became a seminal Swiss Style guide (*Emil Ruder: Typography*).

Josef Müller-Brockmann's 1953 *Mind That Child!* poster is generally cited as the first defining work in the Swiss Style. It featured text set in lower-case Akzidenz Grotesk, photographic images, dramatic distortions of scale and uneasy, intense cropping. The next high-profile example of the Swiss Style came in 1955, when Karl Gerstner was commissioned to design

> *'The formal organisation of the surface by means of the grid, a knowledge of the rules that govern legibility and the meaningful use of colour are among the tools a designer must master ...'*
>
> Josef Muller-Brockmann

and edit a special graphic design issue of architecture/design magazine, *Werk*. Gerstner set all the text ranged left and unjustified, and used an elaborate grid system to lay out the magazine. He described the role of the grid as that of a 'proportional regulator for layout, tables, pictures etc'. Thereafter, the use of the grid became a key characteristic of the Swiss Style.

Along with Akzidenz Grotesk, Swiss Style designers used Paul Renner's Futura and Adrian Frutiger's Univers typefaces, and in 1951, the Haas Foundry in Zurich commissioned Max Meidinger to design a new sans-serif typeface based on Akzidenz Grotesk. The result, Neue Haas Grotesk, was released in 1953. It was later sold to the Stempel Foundry in 1957 and renamed Helvetica.

In 1958, Müller-Brockmann and fellow graphic designer, Hans Neuburg, launched the magazine *Neue Grafik* (*New Graphic Design*), along with archtitect and artist Carlo Virarelli and artist Richard Lohse. The magazine offered an 'international platform for the discussion of modern graphic and applied art' and became a showcase for the Swiss Style. It also introduced the Swiss Style to the American designers, and became hugely influential in the the late 1950s/early 1960s American corporate identity design boom.

Tadanori Yokoo

Once dubbed the 'Andy Warhol of Japan' for the vivid, explosively colourful psychedelia-meets-pop-art posters, book jackets and album covers he designed in the 1960s and 1970s, Tadanori Yokoo remains a major figure in Japanese graphic design and a seminal influence on Western graphic design and pop culture.

Born 1936, Hyugo Prefecture, Japan

Importance Japan's foremost graphic designer of the 1960s and 1970s – a rebel and a legend

Yokoo started out working for a chamber of commerce, replicating paintings and designing wrapping paper and posters. He first came to public attention in 1965 when he designed a poster for an exhibition held at the Matsuya department store in Tokyo. The poster, which imagined a scene from his own funeral – complete with archetypal Japanese imagery including a rising sun, Mount Fuji and the bullet train – is today considered a precursor to the San Francisco hippy-era poster boom of the middle to late 1960s. It is for this reason that Yokoo's work is often compared to that of Victor Moscoso. The poster ushered in Yokoo's vision, which was to combine pop art influences to traditional Japanese woodblock prints, known as *ukiyo-e*.

Yokoo's work has continued to pair his unique approach with traditional Japanese printmaking techniques to this day. Alongside posters, book jackets and album covers, Yokoo also began to direct publicity reels and animated films in the 1960s.

'Modernist design, linked as it has become to modern industry, has made a contribution to our materialistic civilisation. But conversely, it is now trying to rid us of our souls.'

At the end of the 1960s, Yokoo travelled to India and returned with the colourful Indian palette to add to his already vibrant style. His work, a challenge to the prevailing Japanese modernist design styles, led to him being tagged a rebel artist in his native Japan. Conversely, that rebel status brought him prestigious design projects abroad in the late 1960s and 1970s, including designing album covers for The Beatles (*The Beatles*, 1972), Santana (*Lotus*, 1974) and Miles Davis (*Agharta*, 1975).

Such was Yokoo's counter-culture appeal that The Beatles asked him to art direct and animate their 1968 film *Yellow Submarine*. A typically Yokoo vibrant

Yokoo's celebrated 1966 poster, Takarazuka, Grand Revue.

and psychedelic design, the film and his accompanying poster brought him international acclaim and led to his work being included in MoMA's 'Word & Image' exhibition in the same year. Four years later, MoMA opened a solo retrospective of his graphic design work to date.

Yokoo entered the 1980s claiming to have 'retired' from commercial work. The by-then reclusive figure was instead concentrating on painting. He has, however, continued to produce commercial work. Today, he remains a cult legend in Japan and a primary influence on poster design and graphic design at large.

Victor Moscoso

Victor Moscoso's work remains inseparably associated with the psychedelic zenith of the 1960s in San Francisco, with the Filmore music venue at its epicentre. Moscoso's use of what is now known as the 'vibrating colour technique' made for iconic music posters: rich with American 1960s hippy culture and full of vibrant colour, energy and optimism.

Born 1936, La Coruna, Spain
Importance Groundbreaking 1960s psychedelic poster designer

Born in Spain, Moscoso studied at Cooper Union in New York and then at Yale University before switching coasts in 1959 and settling in San Francisco. There, he started teaching graphic design at the San Francisco Art Institute. As the music scene evolved, Moscoso became a regular at venues such as the Avalon Theater, where the flower-power music movement, soon to be internationally-hailed, was gaining momentum. In 1966, at one such event at the Avalon, Moscoso had an epiphany while looking at a rock poster – he felt he could do it better. His first poster project involved a series of concert advertisements for the Avalon venue's Family Dog dance events.

Victor Moscoso in front of his San Francisco apartment door, 1960, which is covered in examples of his work.

There followed an intriguing (and at the time unusual) convergence between Moscoso's academic background and the 'street' art values of the rock poster. Importing to uncharted territory the concept of vibrating colour that he had learned from artist Josef Albers while at Yale, Moscoso designed a series of posters promoting musicians and events, whose designs played imaginatively with optical effects. All posters were printed using offset lithography, which captured 1960s West Coast music perfectly in visual terms, and has since come to define the music in pop culture history.

The vibrating colour technique gave the posters their iconic psychedelic visual language, and was achieved by using colours from the opposite end of the colour wheel (like red and green) and applying them in different degrees of intensity. There were no divisions between the colours, which gave the feeling that all of the colours were competing with one another, leaving the viewer with the sense that there was no one single colour to focus on. In addition to the unique application of vibrating colour, Moscoso brought further pioneering methods to the field, namely the first rock music poster artist to make use of photographic collage.

OFF-SET LITHOGRAPHY
Off-set lithography is today the most commercially prevalent method of printing. A furthering of the principles of lithographic printing, off-set lithography differs in that ink is first transferred to a separate surface before being applied to paper.

Under his own imprint, Neon Rose, Moscoso designed a series of posters for the Matrix, another local venue. His reputation grew and he produced high-profile work for the Filmore venue between 1966 and 1970. Moscoso then gradually moved into designing album covers. His best-known sleeves were designed for Jerry Garcia, Bob Weir and Herbie Hancock. At the same time, he became involved in the Underground Comix scene alongside Robert Crumb. Moscoso's work was a key feature of the *Zap* comic, from its 1968 launch onwards, for which he drew panels, alternating his work with fellow psychedelic American designer, Rick Griffin.

Moscoso continues to work today and remains best known for his iconic psychedelic rock posters, which offer a vivid design snapshot of San Francisco's 1960s musical and cultural hippy epicentre.

Aleksander Rodchenko

Russian artist Aleksander Mikhailovich Rodchenko was a co-founder of the constructivist movement. He remains best known for his pioneering use of photomontage, in which he employed a combination of found and original photographs, often tightly cropped imagery and bold and empowering type to create strong, instantly recognisable compositions.

Born 1891, St Petersburg, Russia
Importance Co-founder of the constructivist movement
Died 1956, Moscow, Russia

Born in St Petersburg, Rodchenko came to attention in the early 1920s as a figurehead of the constructivist movement, conceived with close friend and kindred artistic spirit Vladimir Tatlin and Rodchenko's artist and designer wife, Varvara Stepanova. In 1921, he became a member of an artist's group called the Productivists, which sought to incorporate art into the everyday, reflecting the Soviet ideals of the time. He abandoned painting in favour of commercial graphic design, designing posters, books and films.

In 1923, Rodchenko published his first photomontage: an illustrated poem by his close associate and leading poet, Vladimir Mayakovsky, *Pro Eto* (*About This*). Heavily influenced by the photomontage techniques developed by the German Dadaists, *About This* was Rodchenko's first exploration into using found images in his work (cut out of

Rodchenko's cover for About This *(1923), believed to be the first book design to use photomontage.*

American and European magazines), and featured nine letterpress photomontages. The jacket displayed a stern black-and-white portrait of Mayakovsky's charismatic muse, Lilya Brik, with the author's name and book title rendered in rough-hewn blue and white type. A few years later, he began to shoot his own photographs, eventually working with both found and original photographs in his montages.

Rodchenko taught for 10 years from 1920 to 1930 at the Vysshiye Khudozhestvenno-Tekhnicheskiye Masterskiye (Higher Art and Technical Studios), or Vkhutemas, in Moscow. In 1920, he was appointed the Director of the Museum Bureau and Purchasing Fund. At this time, his views were a clear reflection of Russian communist ideals: that he could change society through his work (art). He was also very much in favour of the nationalisation of industry, even of photography. During this time, Rodchenko also designed many books. He had explored the form as an adolescent, crafting small editions of handmade carbon-copied books, and his pioneering work on *About This* developed this interest.

DADAISM
Dadaism was a European art movement, active between 1916 and 1923, which saw artists such as Kurt Schwitters and Marcel Duchamp and writers, like Tristan Tzara, challenge existing conventions by celebrating ideas of the absurd and nonsense.

In 1928, Rodchenko joined the October circle of artists but was expelled three years later on charges of 'formalism'. Despite photographing symbols of Stalinist Russia, the photographs were seen as overly stylised, leading to accusations of pandering to Westernised ideals, and this in turn led to his expulsion from the group. This marked a significant turning point in Rodchenko's career, resulting in a return to painting in the late 1930s and he eventually ceased all photography from 1942 onwards. While he continued to work after his expulsion, he did so with more caution, being mindful as to who and what he chose as his subjects.

In spite of these unexpected professional turns, Rodchenko's diagonal shots, now known as 'Rodchenko angles', made for strong, sometimes uneasy compositions. They typify Russian constructivism and continue to significantly impact and influence graphic design today.

CONSTRUCTIVISM

Constructivism was a Russian art movement that emerged in 1913. At its heart was the ideal that art should mirror the developments of what was then the new technological landscape. The movement, which initially thrived under the Communist Soviet state, eventually fell out of favour and by the 1940s was all but extinct.

For many Russian artists and designers working in the wake of the Russian Revolution of 1917, the newly founded Soviet Union obliged them to originate radical artistic styles for their new utopian society. With Lenin pronouncing the importance of organisation, machines and labour, these artists and designers sought to create an original form of art that paralleled state development. The result, constructivism, rejected art for art's sake and instead called on art to reflect upon and contribute to society in some way.

In fact, constructivism started four years before the revolution, when sculptor Vladimir Tatlin saw Pablo Picasso's three-dimensional sculptures crafted from wood, paper and other diverse materials, on a visit to Paris. On his return to Moscow, Tatlin was inspired to create, first, relief-paintings, and then sculptures, using materials such as metal, wire, wood, plastic, string and glass. As solid materials entered the process, the construction of the art assumed an elevated significance.

After the revolution, Tatlin was appointed head of the Moscow branch of IZO Narkompros (Visual Arts Department of the Commissariat for People's Enlightenment), where he worked with artists to realise visual media that promoted state propaganda. It was through official state channels, therefore, that Russian constructivist artists found their work functional on a mammoth scale; the heightened visual elements of their art were necessary on account of the degree of illiteracy across the Soviet Union.

The term 'constructivism' was first used by sculptor Naum Gabo and his brother, Antoine Pevsner, in their 'Realistic Manifesto', published in 1920. By then, Gabo and Tatlin were part of a movement that included the artists El Lissitzky and Aleksander Rodchenko. Once the revolution had happened, constructivist art and graphic design flooded the state. The poet Vladimir Mayakovsky created large numbers of single-sided bulletin posters for Rosta, the state agency for transmitting news. Here he created his notorious propaganda poster, *Beat the Whites with the Red Wedge* (see page 99) in 1919, which typified the constructivist style with its geometric shapes, simple use of two colours (red and black), government of white space and crudely produced, stencilled text.

> *'The artist constructs a new symbol with his brush … a symbol of a new world, which is being built upon and which exists by the way of the people.'*
> El Lissitsky

Rodchenko, like other constructivists, embraced photography; the mechanical means of creating an image and its potential for mass production via printing chimed ideologically with State political goals. Rodchenko was the first to experiment with photomontage (see page 68), making it a key distinctive element of the constructivist style. It was Gustav Klutsis, however, whose photomontage-driven political posters promoted Soviet propaganda to the masses.

El Lissitzky's book designs have long been influential. One classic design, of Mayakovsky's book *Dlya Golossa* (1923), contained illustrations crafted from printers' rules and an index code with a symbol for each poem in the collection. Of his lifelong experiments with book design, Lissitzky said, 'The book is the monument of the future.'

By the turn of the 1930s, Socialist realism had become the Soviet State's preferred mode for propaganda and sponsorship of the constructivists quickly diminished.

John Heartfield

The photomontaged illustrations produced by John Heartfield in the 1930s in reaction to the growing power of the Nazi party are the medium's most complex and genuine. Heartfield, an ardent communist and anti-war propagandist, seemed to predict many of the horrors brought on by the fascists and the Second World War. He was a true pioneer in the use of the photomontage, creating biting satires with images that were technically flawless.

Born 1891, Berlin, Germany
Importance Brought technical genius to the art of photomontage
Died 1968, Berlin, Germany

Born Helmut Herzfelde in Germany, Heartfield anglicised his name – in a Dada-spirited act – to protest against the growing anti-English sentiment in Germany that had arisen in response to severe war reparations set by the Allies following Germany's loss in the First World War. Although Heartfield, George Grosz, (fellow German Dadaist and friend) and Gustav Klutsis (Russian constructivist and agitprop designer) all took credit for inventing photomontage, the manipulation of photographs had, in fact, existed since the birth of the medium. The Dadaists and the constructivists simply raised the level of sophistication, complexity and the type and depth of content that could result. For Heartfield and his fellow Dadaists, photomontage also reflected an interest in the machine, the mechanical and the 'modern'. Heartfield stated that the 'new man' must 'paint with photos, draw with photos'.

In 1916, along with his brother Wieland Herzfelde, Heartfield began publishing the anti-war journal *Neue Jugend* (*New Youth*) in which they experimented with radical uses of type and photomontage. With George Grosz, the brothers collaborated at Der Malik Verlag where Heartfield designed many of the covers for leftist literature, including Kurt Tucholsky's *Deutschland, Deutschland über alles* and many books by Upton Sinclair. These remarkable covers often featured photomontages about the working classes and factory workers or poked fun at German nobility. Unlike his fellow German Dadaists, whose theatre and art often depended on randomness, Heartfield's illustrations were anything but accidental; he laboured over them, sometimes in the darkroom for days using multiple exposures and whatever technical tricks he could to make each one appear as perfect a visual metaphor as possible. He most often used his own photographs, frequently dressing up his friends as subjects.

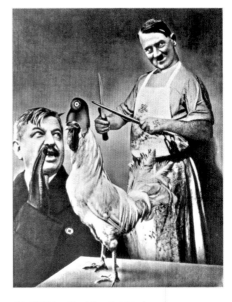

Adolf Hitler: Don't be afraid, he's a vegetarian *(1936) typifies Heartfield's subversive photomontages.*

Heartfield's most powerful and subversive works were created from 1930 to 1938 for the *Arbeiter Illustrierte Zeitung* (*AIZ*, or *Workers Illustrated Journal*) – a publication that had a circulation of a half a million readers at its peak. In these illustrations he savagely satirised the rising power of the Nazis in Germany and warned of the coming violence. *Adolph Swallows Gold and Spouts Garbage*, produced for *AIZ*, is perhaps his most famous image; an almost realistic depiction of an X-ray of Hitler.

Not surprisingly, Heartfield had to leave Germany to escape persecution by Hitler. He fled to Prague in 1933 and then later to London. After the war he returned to East Germany and Leipzig where he worked for the communist government as well as anti-war causes, continuing to make photomontage and graphic works. Heartfield's illustrations are some of the most moving, disturbing and powerful images created in the history of the graphic arts.

Alexei Brodovitch

Best known for his work as art director for the magazine *Harper's Bazaar* – a position he held for over 25 years – Alexei Brodovitch is credited with bringing a European design sensibility to the American magazine model and in doing so, ushering in a modern design approach to fashion and lifestyle magazines around the world.

Born 1898, Ogolitchi, Russia
Importance Set the template for modern magazine design
Died 1971, Le Thor, France

Born in Russia, Brodovitch's intention to study art at the Imperial Art Academy was thwarted by conscription into the Tsarist army. He subsequently fled to Paris with his wife-to-be and family. There, he worked hard to carve out a niche for himself as a graphic designer. Soon his posters, department store advertisements and display designs began to catch the city's attention and earned him awards at events such as the International Exhibition of Decorative Arts in 1925.

In 1930, Brodovitch was invited to teach at the Philadelphia School of Art, where he founded a new advertising programme. Alongside the lecturing post, he undertook freelance commissions, one of which was seen in 1934 by Carmel Snow, who had just become the new editor at *Harper's Bazaar* in New York. Instantly won over by the Russian émigré's work, Snow hired him as the magazine's art director, a position he would hold until 1958.

An avid believer in the power of photography (he published a groundbreaking monograph of his own photographs, *Ballet*, in 1945), Brodovitch set about championing the medium in the magazine and in doing so, set what has since been adopted as a magazine editorial template. He was ever on the lookout for new talent, which he freely introduced to the magazine wherever possible – his first assistant was a very youthful Irving Penn. Later discoveries included Lisette Model, Robert Frank and Richard Avedon. He also

Brodovitch working on a Paris fashion layout for Harper's Bazaar*, 1937.*

commissioned European artists, such as Henri Cartier-Bresson, Brassaï, Man Ray and Salvador Dalì.

By the 1950s, Brodovitch had fine-tuned his minimalist, stripped-down vision for the magazine – talking often of his sensitivity to, and admiration for, sufficient white space on the page. Photographs and typography alike ended up looking and feeling as if they were hovering on the page: models in haute couture floated in a sea of white background while headlines assumed a refined and gentle, although still authorial, presence.

Parallel to his post at *Harper's*, Brodovitch briefly launched a magazine, *Portfolio*, which published just three issues between 1940 and 1950. The lavishly produced magazine, which championed the likes of Paul Rand, Charles Eames and Saul Steinberg, was an expensive playground for Brodovitch, who filled it with sumptuous die-cuts, transparent pages, fold-outs and different stocks. When he left *Harper's* in 1958, Brodovitch dedicated the rest of his working life to teaching. After retiring in 1968, he settled in a tiny village in the south of France, where he died in 1971.

Today, Brodovitch's pioneering take on the role of magazine art director continues to set editorial and design standards for magazines across the globe.

Herbert Matter

In 1936 Herbert Matter emigrated to the United States taking with him first-hand knowledge of the avant-garde movements of Europe and the teachings of Jan Tschichold and the New Typographers (see page 108). He shared with his European contemporaries a predilection for primary colours, sans-serif type, extensive use of the white of the page and an interest in the possibilities of photography, in particular photomontage. His work as a graphic designer and photographer, as well as a teacher, greatly influenced modern American design.

Born 1907, Engelberg, Switzerland
Importance
Introduced European avant-garde movement to the United States
Died 1984, Amagansett, New York, United States

As a young man, Matter studied painting with the French purists, including Le Corbusier, and worked for the famous poster designer A M Cassandre. Some of his earliest and finest commissions were for the Swiss National Tourist Office. This small series of travel posters for Switzerland and resorts such as Pontresina and Engelberg were widely distributed and were among the first purely photographic posters ever produced. Clarity of message was paramount, as were new visual forms made possible by the use of the camera and, like many of the modernists of the period, Matter believed that mechanically reproduced photographs most appropriately expressed the industrial culture of the twentieth century. He was a master in the use of photography, particularly photomontage, cropping pre-existing tourist photos to produce montages in which the figure–ground relationship and the extreme juxtaposition of scale created a dramatic tension. He frequently used these design devices. The effect was further enhanced in his 1935 poster for Pontresina through his own hand tinting, which bestowed the arresting and heroic image with a strange, unnatural colour.

Like the work he later produced in the United States for magazines such as *Arts & Architecture*, *Vogue*, *Fortune*, and for the modern furniture company, Knoll, these early works share a playfulness and sense of experimentation reminiscent of the Dadaist and surrealist movements. Strange combinations and puzzle-like designs contributed to the impact of the advertisements. His 1948 advertisements for Eero Saarinen's moulded plastic chairs for Knoll borrowed heavily from the mobiles of his friend Alexander Calder. These are some of the most sophisticated and kinetic advertisements ever created. Matter had a particular predilection for the use of abstract patterns found in nature, such as woodgrain or breaking waves on a beach. During

One of Matter's acclaimed America Calling *posters (1941).*

the 1950s, his work began to be become more straightforwardly photographic in nature but no less humorous. Perhaps his most famous image is that of his 1955 advertisement for Knoll in which a filthy chimney sweep rests lazily in Eero Saarinen's bright red Womb chair.

In addition to magazine and advertisement work, Matter designed a number of significant logos, including the simple K for Knoll and New Haven Railroad's identity. From 1952 until 1976, he was a professor of design and photography at Yale University, where he helped to influence and shape many generations of American designers, and to define their profession.

Bruno Munari

Italian artist and designer Bruno Munari was associated with the futurist movement that originated in Italy during the early twentieth century. He is best remembered for his playful, humorous and whimsical designs, and for having written and designed over 70 books of both fiction and non-fiction.

Born 1907, Milan, Italy
Importance Prolific designer across many fields of visual arts, notably children's books
Died 1998, Milan, Italy

When he was 18 years old, having moved to Milan from his hometown of Badia Polesine, Munari began to associate himself and his work with futurism after meeting futurist artist Filippo Tommaso Marinetti. Under Marinetti's influence, Munari emerged as a painter, operating within the second generation of futurists.

Entering the 1930s, Munari began working as a graphic designer and photographer, undertaking projects for clients such as Pirelli, IBM, Olivetti and Cinzano. At the same time, he continued to pursue and develop his artwork. In 1932 he created the first of his photograms, which bore the influence of Laszlo Moholo-Nagy and surrealist photographer Man Ray. Three years later, he unveiled his installation, *Useless Machines*, inspired by a Paris meeting with the surrealists André Breton and Louis Aragon. The installation was a development of an earlier work (*Aerial Machines*), conceived as a three-dimensional mobile painting.

A 1965 photomontage, for a Campari advertising campaign.

Munari's design sensibility worked through a vast range of areas: illustration, photomontage and magazine design. Drawing on his installation work and his understanding of objects moving in physical space (the mobile), Munari began to animate his illustrations. He soon became known for bringing his animations to advertising. During the Second World War, Munari worked as a graphic designer for publishers Mondadori, designed the identity for publishing house Einaudi and served as the art director of *Tempo Magazine*.

In 1945, Munari published his first children's book, the now classic *ABC*, written for his son, Alberto, which succeeded in teaching, entertaining and visually stimulating. It would be the first of many children's books to come, each characterised by Munari's bold, simple, colourful illustrations, text and design. His graphic design practice became less of a focus as he moved into industrial, interior, toy and furniture design.

Returning to painting at the end of the decade, Munari exhibited his 'Negative-Positive' paintings in 1950, works of flat colours, any one of which could be interpreted as holding either the foreground or the background. Many said these were mischievous provocations on the theme of perception. Such playfulness continued, for instance, with the cardboard, wood and pliable metal 'travelling sculptures' that Munari created between 1951 and 1958, designed to be light, easily folded and simple to travel with.

Later in life, Munari was preoccupied primarily with travel (repeatedly to Japan, whose culture he felt a profound affinity with), industrial design projects, lecturing and writing and designing books – notably for children. From this passion, he conceived 'Children's Workshops in the Museum', in 1977, an educational concept that travelled the world. Shortly before he died in 1998, he aptly summarised his professional life in the following way: 'inventor, artist, writer, designer, architect, illustrator, player-with-children'.

PHOTOGRAM
A photogram is a photograph created without a camera or lens, by setting an object onto a piece of paper, or film, coated with light-sensitive materials and exposing the treated paper, or film, to light. The area beneath the object remains unexposed to light, while the surrounding surface is exposed. The contrast between the two surfaces creates the photogram.

FUTURISM

Futurism emerged as an art movement in Italy at the turn of the twentieth century, led by Filippo Tommaso Marinetti. It was a celebration of the modern age and called for art, literature, design and music to reflect the developments of today and tomorrow, hence the 'future'.

F uturism was launched when writer Filippo Marinetti published his futurist manifesto on the front page of French newspaper, *Le Figaro*, on 20 February 1909. The manifesto announced a group of artists who aspired to embrace the modern world with all its emerging technology, machines and dynamism, and reject the status quo.

The manifesto – famous for having 11 points for no other reason than 11 was Marinetti's favourite number – contained decrees such as: 'We want to demolish museums and libraries, fight morality', and 'We declare that the splendour of the world has been enriched by a new beauty: the beauty of speed'. Following the manifesto Marinetti and his fellow futurists staged evenings of talks, readings and music.

In Marinetti's 1913 manifesto 'Destruction of Syntax/Imagination without Strings/Words-in-Freedom', he tackled design methods and called for a different kind of revolution: 'I initiate a typographical revolution … The book must be the futurist expression of our futurist thought.' He outlined a futurist vision for how a book should be designed: 'My revolution is aimed at the so-called typographical harmony of the page, which is contrary to the flux and reflux, the leaps and bursts of style that run through the page. On the same page, therefore, we will use three or four colours of ink, or even 20 different typefaces if necessary. For example: italics for a series of similar or swift sensations, bold face for violent onomatopoeias, and so on. With this typographical revolution and this multicoloured variety in the letters I mean to redouble the expressive force of words.'

Marinetti put these ideals into practice for the design of his 1914 book *Zang Tumb Tumb*, in which explosive typographic and visual elements dominated the page.

Two years later, inspired by Marinetti, Francesco Cangiullo created the book *Caffè-Concerto, Alfabeto A Sorpresa*, which used different typefaces within the text to generate images, so exploring the possibility of type as image. In 1919, Marinetti reflected on his book-creating experiments in the book *Les mots en liberté futuristes* (*The Futurist Words in Freedom*). Typographic compositions, some designed on fold-out pages, demonstrated differing typefaces set in various sizes. The book affirmed his commitment to typographic experiments, which he called 'Words in Freedom'.

'It is in Italy that we are issuing this manifesto of ruinous and incendiary violence, by which we today are founding futurism, because we want to deliver Italy from its gangrene of professors, archaeologists, tourist guides and antiquaries.'

Futurist manifesto

Arguably the zenith of the futurists' book-creating explorations was Fortunato Depero's 1927 bolted book, a literal representation of the futurists' infatuation with all things mechanical. Two large bolts bound the pages of the book together. The book had no fixed position for its layout, meaning that, in order to read it sequentially, the reader had to keep rotating the book. The last groundbreaking book designed by the futurists was *Parole in Libertà Futuriste, olfattive, tattili, termiche* (*The Words-in-freedom, Futurist, Olfactive, Tactilist, Thermal*), designed by Marinetti himself. The book was printed on metal sheets and bound with metal.

Various leading figures in the futurist movement were injured or killed during the First World War. The movement did continue after the war, with strong innovations, but with Marinetti's death in 1944, futurism lost its energetic figurehead.

Wim Crouwel

Dutch modernist graphic designer and typographer Wim Crouwel is best known for having founded the Total Design studio in the 1960s, which championed the idea that design should be approached in its totality, embracing as many visual components as possible and making for a more holistic approach to design.

Born 1928, Groningen, the Netherlands
Importance Leading Dutch designer, founding member of 1960s studio Total Design

The son of a draughtsman, Crouwel came to prominence in the 1950s, his work heavily influenced by Swiss Style pioneer Joseph Müller-Brockmann. Having studied fine art, Crouwel began his career working as a painter. He designed his first poster in 1952 and soon found himself moving away from expressionist painting and more towards modernist graphic design. Two years later, he began working as a freelance graphic designer in Amsterdam.

Crouwel began designing for the Van Abbemuseum in 1954, mostly working on exhibition catalogues and posters. He took the strict modernist view that his role as designer was not about interpreting an artist's work, but rather to convey essential information about the artist's work in as clear and functional a way as possible. Avoiding any extraneous use of ornamentation, Crouwel relied on clean, crisp, typographically strong modernist design to visually communicate the work in what he considered to be the most effective way.

In 1963, he teamed up with Benno Wissing, Friso Kramer and Dick and Paul Schwarz to found the studio Total Design, which was unique for several reasons. Firstly, it was the first studio to accept large-scale, multifaceted design commissions from the government as well as working with smaller commercial clients. Total Design was also unique because, as the name suggested, its design approach was to look at design solutions overall, as opposed to designing solutions in isolation. Total Design's first major commission was for the oil company PAM, to overhaul the firm's visual identity. The studio's response was to redesign every aspect of PAM's network of petrol stations, ranging from print to three-dimensional work. The studio gained much recognition for their work for the Stedelijk Museum, also in Amsterdam, for whom Total produced numerous publications (notably catalogues), brochures and invitations using their signature modernist approach, complete with semi-bold grotesque typefaces and a combination of minimalist and bold compositions.

In 1965, Total Design were commissioned to design the signage for Schiphol airport in Amsterdam. The work has since become known as one of the first genuinely comprehensive signing schemes, the airport re-routed with sans-serif lettering and matching arrows.

Crouwel was well known for the typefaces he designed, in particular New Alphabet, which he originally designed in 1967. The idea for the font was more of a theoretical exploration: a hand-drawn font based on a dot matrix system, the face was as high as it was wide, ensuring a good fit into any grid. Unexpectedly, in the 1990s, the New Alphabet began appearing in British style magazines and spurred Crouwel to digitise the font over 30 years later.

Today, Crouwel is still very active in the Dutch design circuit and continues to rely heavily on his functional design ideals.

One of Crouwel's modernist works for the Stedelijk Museum in Amsterdam.

Push Pin Studio

Push Pin Studio was one of the most influential studios to form in New York in the mid-1950s. Representing a young breed of designer looking to offer new alternatives to the seeming rigidity and straight-jacketing of the Swiss Style, many would even go as far as to say that Push Pin Studio was the start of the emerging postmodern approach to graphic design in the United States.

Born (Milton Glaser) 1929, New York City, New York, United States; (Ed Sorel) 1929, New York City, New York, United States; (Seymour Chwast) 1931, New York City, New York, United States

Importance Founders of 1950s Push Pin Studio, pioneers of early postmodern design

The studio was founded in 1954 by Milton Glaser, Seymour Chwast and Ed Sorel – all three of whom were Cooper Union graduates. Glaser (a graphic designer) met Chwast (graphic designer, type designer, illustrator) and Sorel (graphic designer, cartoonist, illustrator) while studying in the late 1940s and early 1950s.

One of the primary aims for Push Pin Studio (encouraged mostly by Glaser and Chwast) was to explore and use styles that were considered visual clichés, generally out of fashion and favour. This included the use of Victorian typography or wooden type or art nouveau decorative elements. Ultimately, reviving these period visuals and repurposing them in a contemporary frame became a bold counterpoint to the otherwise prevailing Swiss Style, and very quickly this move was applauded and celebrated.

The studio designed a publication, the *Push Pin Almanack*, which they sent out as a promotional tool, in order to show their work to potential clients. In 1957, they changed this promotional publication to *Monthly Graphic* and then, in 1961, to *Push Pin Graphic*, a name that stuck for the next 23 years. The *Push Pin Graphic* wasn't a journal as such, but rather a promotional device that, in many ways, followed the irreverent spirit of the Dadaists. Even the name, *Monthly Graphic*, had been irreverent, as the journal most certainly wasn't published on a monthly basis, or even on any sort of regular basis. The inside of *Monthly Graphic* issue 24 was a prime example of a bizarre and eclectic sampling of illustrations, typical of Push Pin Studio's emerging style – mixed with clip art and photographs, arranged in a tidy grid, almost resembling a game, and almost certainly poking fun at the grid.

Push Pin Studio designed everything from book jackets to album covers to adverts, and became so acclaimed in the 1960s that in 1970 they became the focus of an exhibition at the Louvre's

This 1967 poster announcing a tribute to producer Arthur Freed and the musicals he produced, designed by Chwast, showcases the studio's exuberant and playful design ethos.

Musée des Arts Décoratifs in Paris – a first for an American design studio. The golden age came to an end in 1975 when Glaser left the studio to found Milton Glaser Inc, whose triumphs were numerous and included the iconic 1976 I Love NY logo, arguably the single most recognisable, imitated and reproduced piece of graphic design ever produced. In his absence, Chwast persevered, eventually partnering with Alan Peckolick in 1981 to found Pushpin Lubalin Peckolick, which in time truncated its name to the Pushpin Group.

Long before this, however, the group's reputation had been sealed. The rare combination of irreverence, subverting the Swiss Style and introducing eclectic mixes of obsolete graphic styles had established the Push Pin Studio as one of America's first postmodern design studios.

David Carson

David Carson, the Texas-born professional surfer turned graphic designer and art director, injected the world of graphic design with a new freshness and excitement – and some say controversy – during the 1980s and early 1990s, primarily through his designs for surfing magazine *Beach World* and, subsequently, music magazine *Ray Gun*.

Born 1952, Corpus Christi, Texas, United States

Importance Pushed the boundaries of conventional magazine design

Carson studied sociology at San Diego State University, after which he worked as a teacher at Torrey Pines High School, near San Diego, while also a professional surfer at the time. He got his first taste for graphic design in Rapperswil, Switzerland. It was while travelling there that he participated in a three-week graphic design workshop with Swiss graphic designer Hans Rudolph Lutz, who was to become a key influence on Carson thereafter.

Inspired, he began producing experimental designs for *Transworld Skateboarding* magazine while holding down his high school teaching position. In 1988, he left teaching to become art director of *Musician* magazine. A year later, he returned to the West Coast, where he assisted with the launch of short-lived *Beach Culture* magazine (it folded in 1991). For the title, Carson pioneered what has since been called 'dirty typography' – inventive, provocative, at times almost illegible layouts that challenged most rules of graphic design. Even if the magazine wasn't built to last, Carson's design and art direction won the title various design awards. He took the same trailblazing vision to *Surfer* magazine where he worked for a year before leaving, at Malcolm Garrett's invitation, to help launch *Ray Gun* in 1992. It was over the next three years and thirty issues that Carson became an international design 'star', one of the first of his generation.

For *Ray Gun*, Carson pushed all boundaries of magazine design, laying out interviews with bands in such a way that they were barely decipherable and rendering type as if it been drafted, faxed, photocopied and then dragged under the wheels of a bus prior to publication. His approach was often provocative and controversial – he once, infamously, designed an interview with Bryan Ferry (which he considered dull) entirely in pictographic dingbats. The actual transcript appeared at the back of the magazine, very much bringing into question the role of designer as author. In short, editorial and design traditions were collapsed and turned inside out and quickly brought Carson commissions from the likes of *The New York Times* and *Newsweek*.

In 1995, his signature style was celebrated in a monograph titled *The End of Print: the Graphic Design of David Carson*, written by Lewis Blackwell. The book became a seminal influence for emerging graphic designers and sold on an unprecedented scale for a graphic design title: in excess of 200,000 copies, worldwide. A second book, *2nd Sight: Grafik Design After the End of Print*, written by Carson and Blackwell, followed in 1997.

Leaving *Ray Gun* that same year, citing publisher interference, Carson launched David Carson Design, based in New York, and embraced film directing, particularly producing commercials. He took on work for corporate giants like Pepsi Cola, Nike, Toyota, Citibank, Levi Strauss, Microsoft, Budweiser, Armani and bands such as Bush and Nine Inch Nails.

Today, Carson continues to lecture as well as publish books such as *Fotografiks*, *TREK* and the *Book of Probes*, and his work and reputation arguably continue to grow.

Carson combines his surfing roots and his typography in this board created for a charity auction (2008).

Neville Brody

Neville Brody was one of the earliest designers to use the Apple Macintosh computer. Through his experiments while employed as art director for *The Face* magazine – which saw photographs bleeding off the magazine covers, varying scale and direction of type from article to article, and headlines designed in unexpected (often illegible) letterforms – Brody was largely responsible for introducing postmodernism to British graphic design.

Born 1957, Southgate, England
Importance Introduced postmodernism to the consumer at large

In autumn 1976, as the Sex Pistols pushed punk into the British mainstream, Brody began a three-year bachelor of arts graphic design degree at the London College of Printing (LCP – now London College of Communication). Inspired by the growing punk scene, he began to experiment in student projects, one of which saw him rotate Queen Elizabeth's head on a British postage stamp by 90 degrees. His tutors, according to legend, threatened to expel him for his radicalism. Despite warnings that his work was not commercial enough, Brody followed his own path and found frequent outlets for his vision while at LCP, for example, designing a poster for a concert by Pere Ubu. His first-year thesis offered a study of

Brody's period as art director of The Face *was marked by innovative design and layout.*

pop art and Dadaism – a clear indication of his strongest influences and prevailing contexts.

On graduating in 1979, punk was beginning to fade out and 'new wave' was taking its place. Brody began designing record covers, first for the label Rocking Russian and then for Stiff Records. The calibre of his work at Stiff Records led to him being offered the job of art director at Fetish Records. Around this same time, he designed cover art for bands at the forefront of the new wave scene, including Clock DVA, Throbbing Gristle, 23 Skidoo and Depeche Mode.

In 1981, Brody became art director for *The Face*, a new British monthly style magazine, which had launched a year earlier. For the next five years, he led the magazine with his provocative Dada-pop-art-punk-new-wave inspired design vision. Here he pushed the boundaries of legibility, relative to both text and image. He moved on from the magazine in 1986 to take up the position of art director at *Arena*, the men's style magazine, a position he held until 1990.

Midway through his stint at *Arena*, the Victoria and Albert Museum (V&A) in London, staged an exhibition of his work to accompany the publication of Brody's first monograph, *The Graphic Language of Neville Brody* written by Jon Wozencroft. The book went on to become the best-selling design title so far published – a feat topped later by David Carson's *The End of Print* (whose title was taken from a description of Carson's work by Brody). A second book followed in 1994, by which time his own studio, previously named Neville Brody Studio, had been renamed Research Studios.

Clients then and since include the BBC, Sony Playstation, D&AD, Nike, the Barbican, Issey Miyake, ICA, Bonfire Snowboarding, Royal Court Theatre, Kenzo, Dom Perignon and Deutsche Bank. In 2006, Brody undertook a complete redesign of *The Times* newspaper, creating a new font titled Times Modern (replacing Times New Roman).

More than any other British designer, largely owing to his early and progressive experimentations with desktop computer technology, it is thanks to Neville Brody that postmodern design succeeded in reaching and appealing to a broad and wide-ranging audience.

Peter Behrens

Peter Behrens worked successfully as an architect, industrial and graphic designer, as well as a typographer and a proselytiser for modern design. He was an innovator in terms of stressing the importance of the architect and designer to the success of the overall company. Stylistically his architectural, industrial and graphic designs were a clear bridge between the ornate work of Jugendstil and the Vienna Secession and the clarity and functionalism of later German modernism.

Born 1868, Hamburg, Germany
Importance Signalled the coming of a new, modern age
Died 1940, Berlin, Germany

Along with fellow designers and professors Hermann Muthesius, Richard Riemerschmid and Josef Maria Olbrich, Behrens founded the Deutscher Werkbund (German Work Association) in 1907 – a professional coalition of designers and manufacturers dedicated to the improvement and promotion of German design. The Werkbund promoted a closer cooperation between industry and designers as well as a necessary improvement in mechanical production. As Friedrich Naumann wrote, 'The machine must be spiritualised.' Standardisation, even in terms of paper sizes, was promoted.

In 1907, Behrens was appointed the artistic advisor of Allgemeine Elektricitäts-Gesellschaft (AEG). In this role as 'art director' he oversaw all visual aspects of the company from the design of their electrical products, to factories and workers' housing. Significantly, for the first time this also

'Through the mass-production of objects of use corresponding to an aesthically refined order, it is possible to carry taste into the broadest sections of the population.'

included the design of a new corporate identity and all printed materials. A fine example of Behrens's reductivist graphics was his 1910 poster for AEG electric light bulbs in which light spread from a bare bulb like dots of energy, surrounded by a simplified black background and little ornamentation. The many logos Behrens designed for AEG also display this sense of restraint; frequently they feature just lettering.

In addition to the graphic work for AEG, Behrens designed a number of successful typefaces for the foundry Klingspor, including Behrens-Schrift, Behrens-Medieval and Behrens-Antiqua. However, he is possibly most famous for the influential turbine factory that he designed for AEG in 1910. Extending his role as artistic advisor, he was also responsible for the innovation of standardising parts and fixtures for the company's lamps.

By this time Behrens's office was filled with the best of the next generation of modern architects and designers, such as Ludwig Mies van der Rohe, Walter Gropius and Le Corbusier. The breadth and eclectic nature of Peter Behrens's influential career were such that he foreshadowed the manner in which many large contemporary design firms work today – a number of design tasks grouped under one roof. His ideas promoting mass production and standardisation were later fully developed by future designers.

Behrens's input into the AEG turbine factory encompassed external and internal design.

Piet Zwart

Piet Zwart stood out as a key figurehead in the Netherlands design community, working variously as a typographer, interior designer, industrial designer, critic, typographer, photographer and lecturer. So broad-reaching was his influence on design that, in 2000, the Association of Dutch designers named him 'Designer of the Century'.

Born 1885, Zaandijk, the Netherlands
Importance Introduced constructivism and De Stijl to the sphere of advertising
Died: 1977, Leidschendam, the Netherlands

Zwart, who often rejected any kind of designer tag in favour of calling himself a 'form engineer', studied painting, architecture and furniture design at a school of arts and crafts in Amsterdam. Zwart undertook various interior design projects while working as an assistant for architects Jan Wils and H P Berlage. Influenced by meeting graphic designers and by the ideas of the De Stijl movement (of which Wils was a founding member), Zwart turned his focus to experimentation with typography. With no training, and hence no concept of what constituted formal rules of typography, he called himself a 'typotekt', a convergence of typographer and architect.

His first typography commission was for Vickershouse, The Hague. Initially influenced by De Stijl, he began to draw increasingly on the constructivist principles of El Lissitzky, making use of collage and incorporating innovative interpretations of photographic images into his designs and typography. Zwart began to develop his own approach to typography, which prioritised function and favoured primary colours and asymmetrical arrangement. He also began to write, contributing to the design criticism discourse. He insisted that in order to master the overall design it was also important to generate the content.

Zwart's holistic approach worked well for large organisations such as PTT (the Dutch Post, Telegraph and Telephone company) and

Nederlandsche Kabelfabriek (NFK), a Dutch cable factory, who commissioned him to design a catalogue of their products and services. The full-colour, 80-page catalogue was vivid with collage, slogans, alternating primary colours and clever occurrences of repetition. It became emblematic of Zwart's design approach. His triumph was to combine sensibilities and aesthetics from abstract art and the avant-garde and apply them to an industrial catalogue and, in doing so, bring beauty to functionality. This was to be just one of over 250 designs that Zwart undertook for NFK, with whom he forged a long and lasting alliance. Another catalogue designed in 1928, had a beige cover with NFK rendered in strong black capitals within a stark grid of heavy black lines. The simple, functional, direct design typified the Bauhaus style.

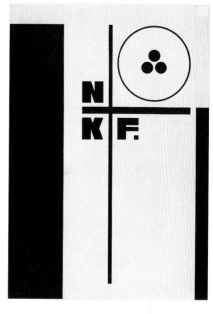

Zwart's 1928 catalogue for NFK is a masterpiece of Bauhaus style.

By the turn of the 1930s, Zwart was one of 12 members of Ring Neue Werbegestalter (literally, circle of new advertising designers), a group formed by artist Kurt Schwitters. Acknowledging his sympathetic functionalist-driven design approach, Zwart was invited to serve as a guest lecturer within the graphic design department at the Bauhaus in Dessau throughout 1931.

Zwart remained active across all disciplines, including interior and furniture design, until his death in 1977 at the age of 92. Today he is revered as a figurehead of modernist typography, and the postgraduate study and research unit of the Willem De Kooning Academy in Rotterdam is named the Piet Zwart Institute – testimony to his incredible influence on graphic design.

Kurt Schwitters

German artist Kurt Schwitters had an illustrious, multidisciplinary career, during which he worked with collage as well as making forays into sculpture, poetry, installation, advertising, typography, performance, photography and architecture, all of which he would later group under the single word 'Merz'.

Born 1887, Hanover, Germany
Importance Dada-inspired conceptual artist and graphic designer
Died 1948, Kendal, England

Schwitters studied at the Dresden School of Art between 1909 and 1914, where his paintings (mostly landscapes) were thought to be thoroughly conventional and pedestrian. Only his final dissertation, an exploration into abstract art, gave any indication of what was to come. On graduating, Schwitters briefly dabbled with impressionism and expressionism before an encounter with Dada artist Hans Arp in Berlin in 1918 introduced Schwitters to Dadaism. Arp, who favoured collage, had a tremendous influence on the young Schwitters, encouraging him to abandon the classical painting strategies he had learnt at art school and instead to embrace the more progressive and daring Dadaist philosophies and practices.

Schwitters returned to Hanover and began to create collage works drawing on the vernacular, using everyday objects such as train tickets, newspaper clippings, postage stamps and waste material. Around the same time, he began to compose Dada-inspired poems using a cut-up technique (later adopted by William S Burroughs) with text made up of newspaper headlines and advertising copy. The most famous, *An Anna Blume,* was published in *Der Sturm*, the leading publication giving voice to the expressionist movement. A collection of Schwitters' writing, *Anna Blume, Dichtungen*, was published in 1919 and sold over 10,000 copies. It was at this time that he started to call his work *Merz* and his collages *Merzbilder* (*Merz* pictures). The word

Merz came from *Kommerz*, German for 'commerce', an ironic, Dada-inspired statement on his own work.

This concept was developed in 1920, when Schwitters set out to construct a cathedral of 'everyday' objects. Initially, it was called the Cathedral of Erotic Misery, then eventually *Merzbau* (*Merz* building). An ever-developing and growing assemblage work, Schwitters continued to add to it, a work always in progress. It included scrap metals, old furniture, a friend's brassiere, pencils – anything he deemed appropriate. It was a statement on the idea that anything could be considered art, drawing on the everyday for a constant source of inspiration.

In 1923, Schwitters began to self-publish a magazine, *Merz*, which lasted until 1932. At the same time, he maintained his own graphic design practice, his commercial work very much influenced by the Russian constructivists. In 1929, he accepted the position of Director of Typography for Dammerstock Estates in Karlsruhe.

In 1937, Schwitters's work fell foul of Hitler's Nazi regime, which pronounced it 'degenerate art', and he fled to Norway. When the Nazis invaded Norway in 1940, he escaped to England, where he was interned for 18 months. Freed, he settled in London. Meanwhile, bombing raids in Hanover destroyed his old studio and the *Merzbau* with it.

Schwitters moved to the Lake District, where, with a grant from MoMA in New York, he began constructing a new *Merzbau*. He died in 1948 and so his work was never finished. Today, Schwitters is seen as one of the forerunners of pioneering graphic design practice.

Schwitters's highly tactile collages, using everyday images, are rooted in Dadaism.

Anton Stankowski

German designer, photographer and painter Anton Stankowski was hailed as master of functionalist graphic design. Producing work that was steeped in the De Stijl and constructivist movements, Stankowski saw no difference between what he called free art (self-initiated or fine art) and applied art (commercial work).

Born 1906, Gelsenkirchen, Germany
Importance Brought an innovative use of photography to design.
Died 1998, Esslingen, Germany

Stankowski grew up in an industrial town and, having briefly followed in the footsteps of most local men by working as a miner, he undertook an apprenticeship with Gelsenkirchen painter and decorator Franz Pusch. He then studied at the Folkwang School of Design in Essen from 1926 to 1927, where tutors such as typographer and poster designer Wilhelm Poetter and interior designer and commercial graphic artist Max Burchartz introduced Stankowski to the ideas and theories of the De Stijl group and the Russian constructivists (see page 40). His work caught the attention of Max Dalang's advertising studio, who invited Stankowski to work for them in Zurich as a photographer.

Stankowski was involved from the outset with commercial design projects and clients liked his style, as he himself explained: 'The objectivity of the photography and minimisation of all subjective elements made this style of advertising very popular among Swiss manufacturers.' His photography saw him experiment with multiple and direct exposure, superimposing and blurring of images, none of which had been seen in the field before. It was during this era, too, that Stankowski introduced his *Theory of Design*, a large collection of his notes on the practice of design.

He lost his residency permit in 1934 and, after working for Swiss clients under the radar for a few years, he returned to Germany in 1938. Settling in Stuttgart, he founded his own studio, Grafische Atelier. Stankowski was then drafted into the army by the Nazis and, after becoming a prisoner-of-war, was only released from captivity in Russia in 1948. Upon his discharge, he worked for *Stuttgarter Illustrierte* as a photographer, editor and designer.

Relaunching his own studio in 1951, his first major project came in 1953 when he designed a celebrated 'halo' logo for the

Stankowski's celebrated Deutsche Bank logo is a triumph of strong corporate identity design.

company, Standard Elektrik Lorenz of Stuttgart. His ability to synthesise the operations agenda of large companies into precise, cleanly-visualised designs, brought Stankowski numerous prestigious corporate logo and identity projects, ranging from work for IBM and REWE through to overseeing the visual identity of the 1972 Olympic Games in Munich. One of his best-known projects, an overhaul of the Deutsche Bank's visual identity in 1974, saw him create an oft-referenced signet that is still in use today, which consisted of a square cut by a single diagonal beam. Steeped in constructivist influence, he invented a new colour palette – known thereafter as 'Deutsche Bank blue'.

Ever drawn to architecture, Stankowksi began to design public spaces and buildings and in the 1960s he designed the 'Berlin layout', a visual identity (including logo) for the city. In the years leading to his death in 1998, he returned to his childhood love of painting. Today, Stankowksi is most often credited for his innovative incorporation of photography within his graphic design practice and for his later constructivist/De Stijl-influenced corporate identity work.

PHOTOMONTAGE

**Photomontage is a technique through which one or more
original and/or found photographic images are combined or
collaged to create a unique, single image. The technique was
popularised as an artistic expression by Dadaists in Berlin,
and also as a political form by Russian constructivists in the
early years of the twentieth century.**

Quite who 'invented' the method of photomontage remains
undecided. Dadaist artist Raoul Hausmann claims to have
invented it in 1918 while holidaying on the Baltic Coast with fellow
Dadaist artist (and partner) Hannah Hoch. In an article titled
'Courier Dada', published in 1958, Hausmann recalled their
discovery, writing, 'In nearly all the homes was found, hung on the
wall, a coloured lithograph representing the image of a grenadier in
front of barracks. In order to make this military memento more
personal, a photographic portrait of the soldier was glued on the
head. It was like a flash, I saw instantly that one could make pictures
composed entirely of cut-up photos.' A 1919 work by the pair, *Cut
With the Kitchen Knife Dada Through the Last Weimar Beer-Belly Epoch in
Germany*, which featured photomontage and collage with watercolour,
is often considered the first recorded work of photomontage.

Artists George Grosz and John Heartfield also claimed to have
invented photomontage in 1916. Grosz is quoted in the 1965 book
Dada: Art and Anti-Art as saying, '(When) Johnny Heartfield and I
invented photomontage in my studio at the south end of the town at
five o'clock one May morning, we had no idea of the immense
possibilities or of the thorny but successful career that awaited the
new invention. On a piece of cardboard we pasted a mishmash of
advertisements for hernia belts, student songbooks and dog food,
labels from schnapps and wine bottles, and photographs from picture

papers, cut up at will in such a way as to say, in pictures, what would have been banned by the censors if we had said it in words.'

Regardless of its precise origin, photomontage was popularised by Berlin-based Dada artists, such as Hausmann, Hoch and Kurt Schwitters. They regarded the medium as a new form representing the chaos of the life surrounding them.

After the Russian Revolution, constructivists inspired by German Dadaist photomontage made explicit the political use of the technique. Gustav Klutsis, in particular, pioneered the use of photomontage when designing state-sponsored Soviet propaganda. His series of postcards for the 1928 All-Union Olympics, are a fine example of Russian constructivist photomontage. Commenting on how the Soviet variation differed from that of Heartfield, Hoch and Hausmann in Germany, Klutsis remarked, 'There are two general tendencies in the development of photomontage: one comes from the American publicity and is exploited by the Dadaists and expressionists – the so-called photomontage of form; the second tendency, that of militant and political photomontage, was created on the soil of the Soviet Union.' Not all photomontage by Russian constructivists was political, however – Aleksander Rodchenko famously experimented with the form from 1923 onwards, working with found photographic images, while El Lissitzky used photomontage to create fine art pieces.

The emergence of photomontage as both an artistic and a political tool also impressed its influence on the Bauhaus school (see page 102), most notably on Laszlo Moholy-Nagy. Acceptance for the art form came in 1931, when it was celebrated with the exhibition 'Fotomontage' in Berlin, in which works by Hoch, Hausmann and Heartfield were exhibited alongside advertisements incorporating photomontage. Collectively they revealed the sheer diversity of the form.

> *'When John Heartfield and I invented photomontage in my South End studio … neither of us had any inkling of its great possibilities…'*
>
> George Grosz.

Paul Rand

Illustrator, educator, advertising guru, designer – Paul Rand is known for his significant contribution to many fields of American graphic design, particularly to those of corporate design and magazine art direction. Above all, he excelled at selling an identity and 'almost single-handedly convinced business that design was an effective tool'.

Born 1914, New York City, New York, United States
Importance Infused American graphic design with European influences
Died 1996, Norwalk, Connecticut, United States

Rand was born Peretz Rosenbaum, to a Jewish family in Brooklyn, New York. His first experiment with graphic design came when he designed and painted signage for his father's grocery shop. Growing up, he was enamoured with art and took night classes at The Pratt Institute from 1929 to 1932, while still a student at high school.

After graduating, he studied at Parsons School of Design and the Art Students League, before finding work as an illustrator with Metro Illustrated Services. Despite his formal training, Rand always pronounced himself self-taught, that his best instruction had come from reading about Russian constructivism (see page 40), Cubism, the Swiss Style (see page 32), German advertising trends and the Bauhaus (in particular the work of Moholy-Nagy, Jan Tschichold, Paul Cézanne and Gustav Jensen) in imported magazines such as *Gebrauchsgraphik* (*Commercial Art*).

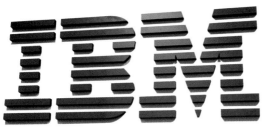

Rand designed the iconic IBM logo of blue striped capital letters in 1956.

In 1935, Rand became a design assistant at George Switzer studio, and changed his name from Peretz Rosenbaum to Paul Rand. He began to gain recognition in 1936 when he became art director at *Apparel Arts* magazine and then *Esquire* magazine. One year later, he designed a logo for Wallace Puppets – a line drawing of a hand dangling the corporate logo as if it were a puppet on strings. The playfulness of the logo marked the beginning of Rand's signature approach: simple and crisp and instantly recognisable.

In 1941, he left *Esquire* to become art director at the William H Weintraub Advertising agency, whose clients included Dunhill, Dubonnet, Olivetti and Coronet Brandy. Rand brought his European influences and advertising know-how together to create powerful corporate design. A typical advertisement from this era was for an Olivetti typewriter, which fused illustration, Swiss Style typography and deliberately rough-hewn constructivist influenced photocollage.

Alongside his new position, Rand also started teaching as a visiting lecturer: first at The Cooper Union and later at The Pratt Institute. As his reputation grew, so did the praise. His artistic mentor Moholy-Nagy said: 'He is an idealist and a realist, using the language of the poet and businessman. He thinks in terms of need and function. He is able to analyse his problems but his fantasy is boundless.'

In 1954, Rand left Weintraub and began working independently. Two years later he began his celebrated stint as a consultant for IBM, a collaboration that lasted until 1991. Subsequent iconic identities were undertaken for American Broadcasting Corporation (ABC) and United Parcel Service of America (UPS).

In 1974, Rand accepted a teaching position at Yale University, a post he held until 1993. He died of cancer just three years later. With his work honoured all over the world, Paul Rand was responsible for numerous recognisable corporate trademarks, seminal books on the subject of graphic design, decades of inspired graduates and many pioneering works of European-influenced American design.

Yusaku Kamekura

In many ways Yusaku Kamekura is the godfather and caretaker of Japanese graphic design, having worked tirelessly during his career to elevate the professional status of graphic design and its practitioners within Japan. In tandem, he created some of Japan's most arresting graphic design images.

Born 1915, Niigata, Japan
Importance Elevated status of Japanese graphic design, establishing its position in global arena
Died 1997, Tokyo, Japan

Kamekura studied at the Institute of New Architecture and Industrial Arts in Tokyo, founded and run by Renshichiro Kawakita. The institute promoted a Russian constructivist and Bauhaus ethos. Kamekura was also influenced by A M Cassandre's art deco poster designs.

On graduating, Kamekura worked as art director for Japanese magazines such as *Nippon* and *Commerce Japan*. In 1951, he helped found the Japan Advertising Arts club, an organisation that is credited with having overhauled public and professional perceptions of graphic design within Japan and put Japanese graphic design on the international radar.

Kamekura's commercial work – designing posters, books, logos, street signs, packaging and advertisements – continued to attract attention. For instance, an advertisement for Fuji Film visually encapsulated Kamekura's constructivist and Bauhaus influences with its use of photomontage,. The piece featured a recurring black-and-white photographic image of a human eye, incorporated with a collaged text and background, that resulted in a vivid and arresting corporate advertisement. Such was the impact of his work, that Kamekura was exhibited at MoMA in New York in 1953.

In 1956, Kamekura's work gained further recognition with his design of the poster *Peacefully Use Atomic Energy*, which won him an award from the Japan Advertising Arts Club. The silkscreen print again displayed Kamekura's trademark constructivist and Bauhaus influenced text and image composition. The result was a functional, simple piece of visual communication.

In 1960, in partnership with Ikko Tanaka, Kamekura founded the Nippon Design Centre in Tokyo, created to rally the Japanese graphic design community and related industries.

Kamekura's work reached an international audience when his identity for the 1964 Tokyo Olympic Games was revealed. In simple functional forms, he juxtaposed the classical icon of the Japanese rising sun with European-influenced type and a vivid image for each poster, whether illustrated or photographic. The concept brought together traditional Eastern and modern Western influences to powerful and arresting effect.

Kamekura's Olympic posters centred on strong images of competing athletes.

In 1978, Kamekura was appointed chairman of the newly launched Japanese Graphic Designers Association. In 1983, he was honoured with an exhibition, 'The Universe of Curved and Straight Lines: Designs by Yusaku Kamekura'. The same year, he created another iconic poster, *Hiroshima Appeals*, for the Hiroshima International Cultural Foundation. The haunting poster depicted falling burning butterflies, a remarkably poignant statement.

Kamekura's legacy remains significant within Japanese graphic design history. His internationally-acclaimed design work and lifelong commitment to developing and helping organisations did much to further the reputation and integrity of Japanese graphic designers.

Film Title Revolutionary
Saul Bass

American graphic designer Saul Bass's pioneering work with film title sequences changed the face and power of what was once considered a pedestrian forum, whose purpose was merely to showcase those who contributed to the making of a film. Instead, Bass re-imagined them as an audience 'conditioner' for what lay ahead.

Born 1920, New York City, New York, United States
Importance Redefined the role of film title sequences within the film industry
Died 1996, Los Angeles, California, United States

Before leaving a firm signature on the film industry, Bass was already a recognised graphic designer. Bronx-born, he studied at the Art Students League in New York and also Brooklyn College, where he was mentored by György Kepes, an émigré Hungarian designer and associate of Laszlo Moholy-Nagy. Kepes introduced Bass to Moholy-Nagy's Bauhaus visions as well as the work of Russian constructivists like Rodchenko. Bass undertook apprenticeships with various Manhattan studios, before breaking out on his own as a freelance designer. In 1946, he moved to Los Angeles to work as art director for advertising agency Buchanan and Company. In 1950, he opened his own studio.

In 1954, film director Otto Preminger, approached Bass to design the poster for his latest film, *Carmen Jones*. Impressed with Bass's work, he proposed that Bass also design the film title sequences for the film. Commissions followed from Robert Aldrich to design the film

A poster for Hitchcock's Vertigo *(1958), showcasing elements of Bass's revolutionary title sequence.*

title sequences for *The Big Knife* (1955), and from Billy Wilder, to do the same for his Marilyn Monroe vehicle, *The Seven Year Itch* (1955).

Then came Bass's groundbreaking moment: Preminger asked him to design the title sequences for his latest film, a risqué adaptation of Nelson Algren's heroin-stricken novel *The Man With The Golden Arm* (1955), starring Frank Sinatra. Bass wanted the titles to set up the film's intentions for the viewer and also serve as a form of prelude to the film's narrative. He designed an animated title sequence, featuring a black paper cutout of an addict's arm – a play on the stereotypical image of the heroin addict injecting the drug. The piece shocked critics and audiences alike.

Bass went on to design many acclaimed title sequences for films such as Alfred Hitchcock's *Vertigo* (1958), *Psycho* (1960) and *North By Northwest* (1959); Otto Preminger's *Bonjour Tristesse* (1958) and *Exodus* (1960); Lewis Milestone's *Ocean's Eleven* (1960); and Stanley Kubrick's *Spartacus* (1960). With John Frankenheimer's *Grand Prix* (1966), he also art directed the racing sequences. In each case, the titles marked the beginning of the film. *Vertigo*, for example, starts with a close-up of Kim Novak's face, then an extreme close-up of her mouth and then her eye. The screen turns red and the film's title explodes, with the type growing larger and larger from her eye.

Following his golden period, Bass moved away from film title design and resumed his commercial graphic design practice, working for clients such as AT&T, Minolta and United Airlines. He was coaxed back to Hollywood, however, and went on to design posters for films such as Stanley Kubrick's *The Shining* (1980) and Steven Spielberg's *Schindler's List* (1993), and title sequences for high-profile films such as James Brooks' *Broadcast News* (1987) and Penny Marshall's *Big* (1988). Most significantly, he worked regularly with Martin Scorsese, designing the titles for *Goodfellas* (1990), *Cape Fear* (1991), *The Age of Innocence* (1993) and *Casino* (1995).

Today, Bass is considered a master and pioneer of the design of film title sequences. He brought art and a sense of narrative to what had previously been a bland functional device.

Otl Aicher

Today, Otl Aicher is best known for leading the team of 40 designers who conceived the globally communicative pictogram-driven design concept for the 1972 Munich Olympic Games.

Born 1922, Ulm, Germany
Importance Famed for designing the identity concept for the 1972 Munich Olympic Games
Died 1991, Rotis über Leutkirch, Germany

Aicher grew up under the shadow of Nazism and was opposed to Hitler's ascension. As a member of the White Rose resistance movement, he acquired a reputation as a dissenter. Once Hitler came to power, Aicher was arrested in 1937 for refusing to enlist in the Hitler Youth movement; he was 15 at the time. The arrest led to him being barred from college entrance exams in 1941 and instead, he was drafted into the German army. In 1945, he deserted and went into hiding in a childhood friend's house.

When the Second World War had ended, Aicher came out of hiding and returned to Ulm, where he was involved in the rebuilding of the city. He founded a series of Thursday night lectures, titled 'Ulmer Kreis' (Ulm Circle of Friends), for which he designed the posters. In doing so, he initiated himself into a lifetime's commitment to graphic design, and he started his own design studio, Bureau Aicher, in 1948. Involved with Ulm's Volkshochschule (Adult Education Institute), Aicher designed their posters and college literature. In 1952, he played an instrumental role in founding the Hochschule für Gestaltung (HfG; University for Art and Design), which went on to become one of the primary German centres for the study of design. Aicher himself lectured in visual communication. As part of the school's student development unit, Aicher and a select group of students, worked on large corporate design projects for clients such as Braun (1954) and Lufthansa (1964).

On account of his pioneering work at the HfG, Aicher was commissioned in 1967 by the National Olympic Committee to create design concepts for the 1972 Olympic Games in Munich. One year later, based on his initial work, he was appointed director of the Olympic design programme, an appointment that involved overseeing a team of more than 40 designers. The appointment was fortuitous as the HfG was to close that year. Using a system of colourful pictograms, Aicher steered his Olympics team to execute a concept that would speak to a multinational, multicultural audience in one simple visual language. While pictograms had been used for the 1948 Olympics in London and again in 1964 for the games in Tokyo, Eicher's pictograms for Munich represented a zenith for the medium because they succeeded in communicating across cultural and linguistic lines in a way that had unprecedented universal appeal.

Thereafter, Aicher moved to Leutkirch im Allgäu, where he set up a new practice, known as Rotis. From there, he continued to work on major corporate identity projects for clients such as German television network, ZDF, ERCO lighting, and household fitting manufacturers, FSB. He also began to write about visual communication, publishing *The Kitchen is for Cooking* in 1982 and *Critique of the Automobile* in 1984.

In 1988, Aicher developed the Rotis font family, which was used for the identity and signage system of the metro in Bilbao – a project in collaboration with Sir Norman Foster. However, his prime achievement remains the design of the 1972 Munich Olympic Games, using a single system of colourful pictograms to transcend the world's cultural and language barriers.

Aicher and team's highly acclaimed pictograms for the 1972 Olympics.

Karl Gerstner

Karl Gerstner is one of the most important and influential Swiss graphic designers, a figurehead in what has come to be known as the 'second wave' of the Swiss Style. Among his achievements are the creation of a flexible grid , the promotion of integral typography and the use of text set left and unjustified. He also launched and grew a successful global advertising agency.

Born 1930, Basel, Switzerland
Importance Seminal second-wave Swiss Style designer

Gerstner took his art foundation at the Kunstgewerbeschule (School of Design), in his hometown of Basel, studying under Emil Ruder, a pioneer of the Swiss Style that emerged between the Second World War and the end of the cold war (see page 32). He had arrived there through unfortunate circumstances: he had wanted to study to be a chemist, but his parents could not afford the tuition so, instead, he took the one-year foundation course. The programme instructed him in the skills and ideology of the Swiss Style, which Gerstner was eager to acquire. Upon graduating he took an apprenticeship with graphic designer and artist Fritz Buhler where he met Armin Hofmann, who would also

A 1960 advertisement for Schwitter AG, demonstrating the use of set left text.

later teach with Ruder at the Kunstgewerbeschule. Hofmann taught Gerstner about the Bauhaus, which was to form a major influence.

At the end of his apprenticeship, Gerstner became a freelance designer, working for Geigy chemicals and Schwitter AG, a plate maker. Throughout all of his work lay the influence of the Swiss Style, the Bauhaus and the most recent movement to capture his interest – Art Concret. In his early work he often used the Akzidenz Grotesk typeface and arranged text in unjustified columns. Setting the text in two columns, asymmetrically, to the right-hand side of each page, Gerstner claimed this layout method to be new at the time. Sometimes Gerstner, who was also a painter, incorporated his own abstract paintings into his designs. He would go on to find considerable recognition with his paintings – his first solo exhibition was staged in 1957.

In 1955, Gerstner got his big break when he was invited to design and edit an entire issue of *Werk* magazine (literally, *Work*). Using unjustified text and an elaborate grid, Gerstner based the issue entirely on the Swiss Style. Two years later, he began working with copywriter and novelist Markus Kutter. Gerstner designed Kutter's novel *Ship to Europe*, a riot of typographic innovation and experimentation, held together by a tight use of the grid.

In 1959, Gerstner and Kutter founded the agency Gerstner + Kutter Advertising, Graphic Design & Public Relations. The naming of the agency was a statement in itself – the majority of Swiss Style designers avoided the realm of advertising, while Gerstner was keen to embrace it. In 1962, they were joined by Paul Gredinger, an architect whose role was to court industrial design projects, after which the agency's name changed to GGK. The agency went on to become one of the most internationally recognised in the world, winning the Ford account in 1968 and relocating to Dusseldorf, where Ford's headquarters were. By the mid-1970s, the firm counted Ford, Volkswagen, IBM Europe and Swiss Air among their prestigious clients.

ART CONCRET
Art Concret is an abstract art movement. The term was coined in 1930 by Dutch artist Theo van Doesburg in his Manifesto of Concrete Art, which called for a new abstract art without symbolic associations.

Pentagram

The self-described 'multidisciplinary design firm' Pentagram was founded in London in 1972 by three graphic designers, an industrial designer and an architect. Employing over 200 staff today, the company now has several offices worldwide, each with teams whose members continue to be diverse in discipline and talent, yet work side by side.

Born (Theo Crosby) 1925, South Africa; (Colin Forbes) 1928, London, England; (Kenneth Grange) 1929, London, England; (Alan Fletcher) 1931, Nairobi, Kenya; (Mervyn Kurlansky) 1936, Johannesburg, South Africa

Importance The first truly multidisciplinary design firm

Died: (Theo Crosby) 1994, London, England; (Alan Fletcher) 2006, East Sussex, England

The firm started out in a studio on Needham Road, in London's Notting Hill. The founding partners were Alan Fletcher, Theo Crosby, Colin Forbes, Kenneth Grange and Mervyn Kurlansky.

Alan Fletcher, born in Kenya, grew up in London's Shepherd's Bush. In 1956, he began studying at the Royal College of Art (RCA). Disheartened by London's post-war dreariness, he finished his studies at Yale School of Art and Design on a scholarship. Studying under the likes of Paul Rand and Josef Albers while at Yale, Fletcher stayed in the United States for the next few years and found himself working with Saul Bass and Leo Lionni on graduating.

Fletcher returned to London in 1959 and, with former RCA classmate Colin Forbes and American designer Bob Gill, set up Fletcher Forbes Gill. The studio combined Fletcher's iconic sense of humour and wit with the others' Swiss modernist restrained design approach. It was not long before they established their reputation. Working for the likes of Pirelli slippers (Fletcher Forbes Gill's bus-side campaign where passengers appeared to be wearing slippers) and Shell Petroleum (proposing to use the furniture in Shell garages to spell out the word 'shell') managed to put the studio firmly on the London design map.

In 1965, Gill left the popular partnership, going freelance as an independent. In his place, came the architect Theo Crosby and the studio was renamed Crosby, Fletcher, Forbes. Major projects for Penguin, Shell and Reuters followed. As demand for their services outstripped their manpower, at the turn of the 1970's, they brought in industrial designer Kenneth Grange and designer Mervyn Kurlansky. In 1972, Fletcher overhauled the studio as an independent five partner multidisciplinary agency. They renamed themselves Pentagram. They believed that 'big companies would be more interested in dealing with organisations than with individuals'. This meant that the studio had no pyramid management structure and that there was equality in salary, decision-making and input, values which Pentagram uphold to this day.

Pentagram redrew the iconic Penguin Books logo and provided new guidelines for its use as part of a wider identity management programme in 2003.

Pentagram cemented a definitive, understated and restrained design approach and displayed a rare ability to combine a sense of play and lightness of touch and wit when dealing with large corporate identities and clients. In 1978, Forbes formed the New York office, a move led to the studio becoming an international success. The firm's commercial design success stands testimony to this, with a wide range of clients including Kodak, Penguin Books, British Airways and Saks Fifth Avenue. Pentagram's unique business model and original approach continue to make a mark on graphic design history.

Today, only Forbes remains as a partner in the firm. Recently, Pentagram has demonstrated its commitment to social design issues and initiatives, incorporating pro-bono services for the likes of One Laptop per Child. This is a clear indication that Pentagram not only continues to be relevant, but also always stays one step ahead of the game.

Massimo Vignelli

Although credited with a diverse range of work, Massimo Vignelli remains best known for his work in the field of transportation graphics, notably his iconic design of the subway signage and maps for the New York Metropolitan Transportation Authority and the transportation signage system for the Metropolitan Area Transit Authority of Washington DC.

Born 1931, Milan, Italy
Importance Designer of the New York City subway map and signage

Vignelli studied architecture at the Politecnico di Milano between 1950 and 1953, before going on to study at Università di Architettura in Venice. It was there that he met his lifelong creative, business and romantic partner Lella Valle. At the time, Massimo was also working for Venini Glass as a glass designer. In 1955, he designed the 'Fungo' lamp, inspired by the shape of a mushroom. He married Lella in 1957, and they spent two years living in the United States, Massimo having been invited to take up a fellowship at the Chicago Institute of Design. During this time, Lella worked for New York firm of architects Skidmore, Owings & Merrill.

In 1960, the designer and architect duo returned to Milan and opened their own firm, billed as an 'office of design and architecture'. Their key clients included Pirelli, Rank Zerox and Olivetti. In 1965, Massimo teamed up with Jay Doblin and Bob Noorda to found a design studio called Unimark International. Later that same

'There are three investigations in design. The first is the search for structure. Its reward is discipline. The second is the search for specificity. This yields appropriateness. Finally, we search for fun, and we create ambiguity.'

year, the Vignellis moved permanently to New York, where they opened a new Unimark office, specialising in corporate identity design. Six years later, they unveiled a new husband-and-wife studio, Vignelli Associates, which is still active today. Their clients from that time on have included Rank Xerox, McGraw Hill, Ford Motor Co, American Airlines, Bloomingdale's, the Guggenheim Museum, IBM, Pirelli and MoMA. Alongside the studio's work, both Vignellis continued to be active in furniture and product design.

In 1972, Vignelli Associates took on what would become their most iconic project to date: a brand new design of the New York City subway map and a system of signage for the subway itself. As with Harry Beck's 1933 London Underground map, Vignelli set about designing his subway map without feeling obliged to represent the literal geography of New York. Instead, he assigned line colours and station dots, reconceiving the original New York subway map as a far clearer network of brightly coloured wiring. Vignelli's map was introduced in 1972 but replaced in 1979 by a literal map that showed New York's precise geography. Many felt that Vignelli's expert work of communication design had been wrongly passed over for a document that communicated far less clearly and effectively.

The Vignellis continue to be admired for their cross-disciplinary design work, which encompasses everything from graphic design to exhibition and furniture design. The critic Paul Goldberger described the Vignellis as 'total designers', which neatly captures the spirit of the design couple.

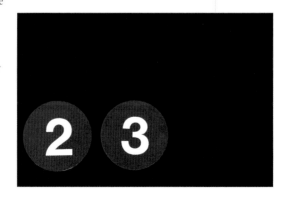

Vignelli's signage for the New York City subway system is renowned for its clarity and ease of use.

Chermayeff and Geismar

The partnership formed in the late 1950s by Ivan Chermayeff and Tom Geismar, arguably set the blueprint for all corporate identity design. Whether working for Mobil, Chase Manhattan Bank or Xerox, the studio today has a portfolio featuring an impressive roster of high-profile corporate identity design projects.

Born (Chermayeff) 1932, London, England; (Geismar), 1931, Glen Ridge, New Jersey, United States
Importance Pioneering corporate identity designers of iconic logos

Geismar, a graphic designer, studied at Rhode Island School of Design and also Brown University before attaining an MA in graphic design from Yale. Chermayeff, an illustrator, designer and artist, studied at Harvard University, the Institute of Design in Chicago and Yale University's School of Art and Architecture. Geismar was from New Jersey, Chermayeff from London – the son of architect, Serge Chermayeff. The two met at Yale, striking up a friendship while working on an assignment about typeface design. After graduating, Geismar served in the army, designing graphics and exhibitions, while Chermayeff designed album cover art for CBS records in New York. Reunited after Geismar's service, they opened their own studio in 1957.

Chermayeff and Geismar were united by a shared belief in the modernist creed that design must solve problems. In practical terms, this meant they paid enormous attention to the creative process. The pair believed then, as now, that graphic design is about linking the information that needs to be communicated with a design that will best articulate and present that information.

Initially competing for business against seminal American designers of the time, including Saul Bass and Paul Rand, the studio secured its own niche when it designed a corporate logo for Chase Manhattan Bank. The symbol, four blue interlocking pieces, in the

Chermayeff and Geismar's logo for Mobil remains a graphic design classic.

shape of an octagon, contains no mention of the company name. It is crisp, iconic and entirely visual, without any text.

Chermayeff and Geismar would go on to design less abstract, but no less powerful, iconic symbols and logos for the likes of NBC, Pan Am, Harper Collins, Mobil and Zerox – all of which are internationally and instantly visually recognisable to so many people today.

When the Manhattan department store Barney's wanted to enhance its identity, Chermayeff and Geismar removed the apostrophe, rendering Barney's as 'Barneys', and then added 'New York' to the logo, so the store became 'Barneys New York'. Using clean typography and contributing to the logo's overall brand identity, the redesign succeeded in transforming public perception of the department store.

Similarly, when New York University (NYU) commissioned a new identity, Chermayeff and Geismar designed a logo with a white torch on a blue background. Forty years later, that same symbol remains just as potent. Most recognisable of all, however, remains their logo for Mobil – that clean, crisp unforgettable logo on a white background, with all letters in blue, apart from the 'o' in red.

Unrivalled masters of functional and playful visual communication, Chermayeff and Geismar continue to boast one of the largest portfolios of American corporate identity design today, having secured their place in graphic design history with some of the most recognisable American logotypes of their time.

CORPORATE IDENTITY

Corporate identity design came into its own in the 1950s and 1960s, particularly in the United States, once the Swiss Style had penetrated the graphic design mainstream, giving designers a method through which they could reassess and redesign the identities of large corporations.

The emergence of corporate identity design as an art form is thought to have taken place in 1936 when Walter Paepcke, owner of the Container Corporation of America (CCA), a mass-producer of cardboard boxes, needed to reconsider the visual identity of its promotional and packaging materials. He employed Egbert Jacobson, head of the firm's design department, to draw up an entirely new visual identity. Jacobson, who in his day-to-day work for CCA oversaw stationery, annual reports, invoices and logos, as well as the identity of the offices, factories and transportation vehicles, concieved a new CCA logo that set the firm's initials in a grotesque typeface within a hexagon. Paepcke responded by having Jacobson roll out the new logo design across all aspects of the corporation's identity and, in doing so, set a trend for corporations to assess their identity holistically. Paepcke and Jacobson

'We try to do something that is memorable for a symbol. Something that has some barb to it that will make it stick in your mind, make it different from the others, perhaps unique. And we want to make it attractive, pleasant and appropriate. The challenge is to combine all those things into something simple.'

Tom Geismar

commissioned an advertising agency to design a campaign. The result of this was a series of posters (the 'Great Ideas' posters), each of which was designed by a European or American designer, such as A M Cassandre, Herbert Matter, Herbert Bayer and Laszlo Moholy-Nagy. The series succeeded in importing the European influences of the Bauhaus and Swiss Style (see pages 102 and 32) into the American mainstream.

After the Second World War, the Swiss Style actively inspired many American graphic designers to approach the relationship between business and design differently. The view that a product's mass marketing was no longer something to be suspicious of paved the way for new agendas: corporations now needed to be savvy in terms of visual branding and communication. Firms such as Olivetti and CCA had set the trend for powerful corporate identity systems and now others wanted to follow suit. Corporate giant IBM, fearing Olivetti were soaring ahead of them, hired designer Eliot Noyes as Consultant Director of Design in 1956. He subsequently brought in Charles Eames to consult on product designs and Paul Rand as graphic designer. That year, Rand sealed his destiny as one of the world's most acclaimed corporate identity designers by designing the iconic IBM logo using block letters in the City Medium typeface (see page 70).

By the 1960s, corporations were all striving for potent universal identities and corporate identity design underwent a boom. Chermayeff and Geismar entered the field on a grand scale with their 1960 overhaul of Chase Manhattan bank, redesigning the firm's logo as an image of abstract, blue geometric shapes. The agency became known internationally for their logo designs, with subsequent iconic logos for Pan Am, Mobil and Xerox.

Paul Rand remained the other leading light of the field, designing logos for corporate clients such as UPS, Enron and American Broadcasting Company (ABC). Following Rand's and Chermayeff and Geismar's incredible run, the golden boom of corporate design settled down to become an integral, obvious part of both the business and design arena.

Gert Dumbar

Gert Dumbar, who runs his own Studio Dumbar, has a reputation for being a renegade – slightly provocative and controversial. Ranging from a quirky redesign of the Dutch postal system to the use of three-dimensional typography or a proliferation of decorative elements – for example , dots – Dumbar's work has proved hugely influential and much imitated in the world of contemporary graphic designy.

Born 1940, Jakarta, Indonesia
Importance Founder of Studio Dumbar, home of quirky, innovative Dutch design

Dumbar was born in Indonesia in 1940, and partly raised there, before his family moved back to the Netherlands. He began his education by studying painting at the Royal Academy of Fine Arts in The Hague, before falling under the influence of Dutch designer Paul Schuitema, who encouraged him to abandon painting for graphic design. For his postgraduate studies, Dumbar moved to London, where he studied graphic design at the Royal College of Art, then under the direction of designer Anthony Froshaug.

Back in the Netherlands, in 1977 Dumbar launched his studio. Around this time, graphic design had very much become a part of everyday life in Europe. Dutch design had begun to command an international respect and reputation, but it wasn't until the 1980s – in large part thanks to Studio Dumbar – that it really began to come into its own. Always priding itself on having a style that is not a style, the studio instead became known for the decorative devices it employed, such as Dumbar's instantly recognisable dots (branded 'measles' by his critics). Constantly moving on from one such device to another, the innovative designs generated at the studio were always fresh.

Always one to challenge conventions and traditional approaches, Dumbar pushed the boundaries of poster design with his 1982 poster

Studio Dumbar has a longstanding design relationship with the Dutch telecoms company, including logo design and visual identity management.

for an American exhibition of the De Stijl movement. Rather than reproducing artwork from the exhibition for the poster, and adding type relative to the work, Dumbar created the first of his 'scene' photographs. He set up a scene in the museum showing the artwork on the wall and a dummy of the artist in front of it. Many considered this to be a sort of visual joke, poking fun at the typically serious and functional tone of exhibition posters.

Since June 2000, Dumbar has been working as a visiting professor at the Royal College of Art, returning to his own postgraduate course programme. He has also periodically been teaching in Indonesia and regularly speaks at design conferences and universities around the world. His reputation as a maverick and renegade Dutch designer continues to grow. When talking about the unique spirit particular to his studio, Dumbar has said, 'I travel a lot and I visit a lot of other design bureaus. And it always strikes me to see how much less hierarchical Studio Dumbar is in comparison. In many design bureaus you see a few stars surrounded by an army of slaves who work out their sketches. Nothing of the kind has ever happened at Studio Dumbar! We cherish the originality of the individual designers; they produce concepts and sketches and then [we] give our fatherly comments.'

April Greiman

When Apple unveiled their first Macintosh computer, most graphic designers were firmly against incorporating the new computer technology into their existing practice; they saw the crude performance of what was then primitive software as an obstacle to the modernist approach. Going against mainstream opinion, April Greiman saw exactly the opposite and considered the potential to be limitless.

Born 1948, New York City, New York, United States
Importance One of the first graphic designers to boldly embrace computer technology

Greiman was born in 1948 and came to graphic design via a happy accident. She had been intent on studying art at the Rhode Island School of Design (RISD). However, whilst disparaging her drawing skills, the Dean of Admissions flagged up a natural talent for and leaning towards graphics, and recommended that she apply instead to the graphic design programme at the Kansas City Art Institute (KCAI).

Greiman studied under Chris Zelinsky, Inge Druckrey and Hans Allemann, all three of whom were graduates of the Kunstgewerbeschule (School of Design) in Basel, Switzerland, and had strong modernist leanings. Under their mentorship, she attended graduate school in Basel, where she studied under Wolfgang Weingart and

Greiman's lecture poster shows her experimentation with pixellated imagery.

Armin Hofmann. At the time, Weingart's work was moving the Swiss Style towards New Wave (see pages 32 and 124), which exploded formal concepts of how text should appear on a page. These typographical adventures (such as no paragraph indentations, suddenly changing typeface within a word or putting unusually severe spaces between letters) appealed to Greiman, who brought these influences back to the United States.

Settling in Los Angeles, Greiman opened her own studio, Made In Space. In the late 1970s and early 1980s, she pioneered the Swiss New Wave style and is today credited with introducing the irreverent approach to the American design community.

In 1982, Greiman became director of CalArts design programme at the Californinia Institute of the Arts, where she explored new media pathways, working with the latest video and analogue equipment. In 1984, foreseeing graphic design and new media technologies intersecting, Greiman argued strongly to have the CalArts Graphic Design department renamed the Visual Communications Department.

Embracing the Macintosh computer within her new media explorations, Greiman went on to blaze a unique path. Where others feared the image reductivity of computer-generated pixellation, Greiman experimented. In 1984, she designed a poster for industrial designer Ron Rezek, called *Iris Light*, which combined New Wave methods and an innovative still-video image. The result, a hybrid, offered a perfect example of where Greiman saw design heading.

She put her new media adventures to best effect in 1986 when she used the Macintosh to design an issue of *Design Quarterly*, a journal published by the Walker Art Centre in Minneapolis. The issue, entitled 'Does It Make Sense?', is today considered the moment at which computer technology and graphic design intersected, to striking effect. Greiman designed the issue as a 90 x 180 cm (3 x 6 ft) fold-out poster, featuring a digitally manipulated naked self-portrait.

Today, April Greiman is acclaimed as a pioneer of technology-driven graphic design practice, and is widely noted as one of the most accomplished female designers in the industry.

Filippo Tommaso Marinetti

Filippo Tommaso Marinetti was the founder of the futurist movement that emerged in Italy in the 1920s, and became its foremost typographer and propagandist. His 'Free-word Poems' remain some of the most important typographic experiments of the entire century.

Born 1876, Alexandria, Egypt
Importance Freed type from its gridded shackles
Died 1944, Bellagio, Italy

The political and social upheaval that engulfed Europe between the two World Wars created radical changes in the fine arts and the commercial arts. No field was more greatly affected than graphic design, which began to transform itself into the very kind of practice that we think of today. A considerable shift, or revolution, took place in the profession, which saw the designer moving away from being someone vested in the fine arts and draughtsmanship, and towards the more modern concept of being an 'assembler', or as the Dadaists liked to call themselves, a '*monteur*' or mechanic. Marinetti and his loosely organised group of Italian futurists were some of the first to proselytise for, and expand the possibilities of, the graphic arts. Among the significant formal elements introduced to the profession during this period were basic collage techniques and the new use of type as an expressive element in and of itself.

Marinetti was an adept propagandist, and in his first 'Futurist Manifesto' of 1910, published in the newspaper *Le Figaro*, he proclaimed, 'Destroy the cult of the past… totally invalidate all kinds of imitation, elevate all attempts at originality… sweep the whole field of art clean of all themes and subjects which have been used in the past.' He achieved much of this in his famous page from *Free-word Poems*, roughly titled, 'In the evening she read the letter from her artillery man at the front', in which a young woman reads a letter from her husband, brother or boyfriend and experiences, in a moment of 'simultaneity', the artillery exploding over her head. Remarkably, by employing a mix of multiple typefaces and sizes, the chaotic type seemed to explode visually, creating a 'visible poem.'

Although experiments with word poems – in which the words take on their own communicative and illustrative form – had existed since ancient Greece, the necessary but restrictive type layout in the form of a grid had persisted as a mainstay of publishing since Gutenberg invented the printing press in the 1450s. Conveniently, Marinetti lived above a print shop in Rome and glued the letterforms down to a sheet of wood, so eliminating the confines of the ordered letterpress.

The futurists hoped to completely reject the past in favour of a new world based on the 'wisdom' of technology and science. Harmony was dismissed in favour of destruction, turbulence and upheaval; war was positive in that it could wipe the slate clean, creating a *tabla rasa* from which to build. Marinetti, who had been trained as a lawyer at the Sorbonne in Paris, was uniquely qualified to be the main propagandist for this radical movement.

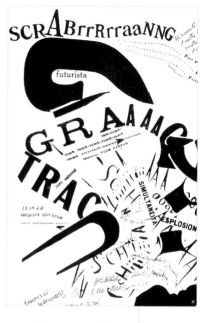

A page from Marinetti's book Words in Liberty (1919) *shows his freedom from the grid.*

In Marinetti's revolutionary *Free-word Poems*, whose very title suggested that words had somehow previously been imprisoned, he introduced a form of collage that allowed and introduced an infinite range of possibilities and expressions for future designers. His ideas helped to free designers from nineteenth-century confines and set the stage for the modernists' adoration of the machine and functionalism.

Paul Renner

Paul Renner is best known for having designed the sans-serif typeface Futura, between the years of 1924 and 1926. Its shapes are today seen as emblematic of the Bauhaus design style that thrived between 1919 and 1933.

Born 1878, Wernigerode, Germany
Importance Typographer best known for designing the typeface Futura
Died 1956, Hödingen, Germany

Renner grew up as one of five sons of a theologian. After studying Greek and Latin, he took an interest in painting. This led him to study art, finishing his education in 1900. Married, he settled in Munich and made his living undertaking painting commissions, including a series of landscapes for the magazine, *Simplicissimus.* When his wife became pregnant in 1907, he sought a steady income and was hired as a book designer for Georg Müller Verlag. He worked there until 1917, designing almost 300 titles in one prolific year. The work tuned his eye to attain balance and rhythm between illustration and typography. In 1911, he co-founded a school for the study of illustration in Munich.

Aa Bb Cc Dd
Ee Ff Gg Hh

Renner's most famous typeface, Futura, remains popular today.

In 1922, Renner published contemplations on his years of experience working as a book designer, in the form of the book *Typografie als Kunst* (*Typography as Art*), which set down clear guidelines on recommended methods and strategies of book design.

In 1924, Renner began his most celebrated endeavour, the creation of the typeface Futura, which he developed over the next two years. His motivation was a desire to marry the Gothic typefaces that were popular in Germany at the time, with a new roman-inspired typeface. The result was a classic, geometric sans-serif typeface with no decorative elements. As its name suggested, it represented a departure from the arts and crafts era and the advent of the modern age. Commissioned by the Bauer type foundry, it was released in 1927. Its modern, unfussy appearance became associated with Bauhaus ideology, even though Renner was not affiliated to the school himself. The font is now considered to be a core example of the so-called New Typography style known as 'geometrical modernism'.

Starting from 1925, Renner became head of the Printing Trade School in Munich, and director of the Master School for Germany's Printers, which he co-founded. He taught alongside friend and colleague Jan Tschichold, a fellow typographer. In 1928, Renner followed Futura with another acclaimed typeface, Plak.

In 1932, Renner failed to find a publisher for a booklet titled *Kulturbolschewismus* (*Cultural Bolshevism*), which critiqued the Nazis' policies relating to culture. Eventually, a Swiss friend published it. As a result, in 1933 Renner was dismissed from his teaching position and dubbed a subversive. That same year, the Nazis shut down the Bauhaus group in Berlin, and Renner's booklet was withdrawn from circulation.

Until his death in 1956, Renner focused primarily on his painting as well as his writing about typography, though he did design further typefaces including Ballade in 1938 and the Steile Futura typeface in 1954.

Renner's contributions to the field of typography are profound. In particular, he is hailed as having single-handedly set the standards for book design and typesetting in Germany during the interwar years.

Eric Gill

Eric Gill was a pioneering British typeface designer and is most recognised for his design of Gill Sans and Perpetua typefaces. He moved seamlessly between his work as sculptor, stone mason, book designer, typeface designer and typesetter.

Born 1882, Brighton, England
Importance Created seminal Gill Sans and Perpetua typefaces
Died 1940, Uxbridge, England

Gill was born in Brighton and studied at the Chichester Technical and Art school. He began an apprenticeship with W D Caroe, a firm that worked in ecclesiastical architecture. In his spare time, Gill studed stone masonry at the Westminster Technical Institute and then calligraphy at the Central School of Arts and Crafts. It was while studying calligraphy that he met, and became heavily influenced by, author and calligrapher Edward Johnston. Gill left W D Caroe in 1903 to pursue a three-pronged career as a monumental mason, letter cutter and calligrapher. He also began to sculpt, and in 1914 he was commissioned to create relief sculptures for the Stations of the Cross at Westminster Cathedral.

A meeting with the typographer Stanley Morrison reignited Gill's interest in type and after moving to Wales in 1924, he set up a new workshop. A year later, he designed the Perpetua Roman typeface. The project was initiated by Stanley Morrison, who was working at the Monotype Corporation, the pioneering typeface design and typesetting company. Gill's inspiration for Perpetua came from designs of old engravings, which manifested in the font's inherent chiselled quality. It is considered to be particularly distinctive for its angular, almost diagonal serifs and also for its medieval numbers.

In 1927, Gill designed another seminal typeface, Gill Sans Serif, inspired by Edward Johnston's sans-serif London Underground typeface. Known as Johnston Sans, this humanist typeface had capital

Aa Bb Cc Dd Ee Ff Gg Hh
Ii Jj Kk Ll Mm Nn Oo Pp
Qq Rr Ss Tt Uu Vv Ww
Xx Yy Zz   1234567890

Like many of his typefaces, Perpetua was inspired by Gill's work with stone.

letters that were based on the Roman letters and were squared off, while the lower-case letters were based on what it known as humanist miniscule, itself inspired by handwriting typically used in fifteenth-century Italy. Sharing characteristics with Gill's later Joanna typeface, Gill Sans was instantly recognisable owing to what some described as the 'eyeglass' lower-case 'g'. Not only did the font work well in varied point sizes, but it also had a good variety of weights, making it easily adaptable. It has since become a British design classic.

In 1928, Gill left Wales, and set up a new printing press and lettering workshop close to High Wycombe in Buckinghamshire, closer to his London client base. There, he designed his next significant typeface, Joanna, a book typeface with small and elegant serifs.

In the last years of his life, Gill worked across different media, producing a group of sculptures for the BBC's Broadcasting House in 1932, designing a stamp for the Post Office in 1937 and, most significantly, creating a series of stone reliefs for the League of Nations headquarters in Geneva. Despite so many accomplishments in so many fields, when Gill died in 1940, his headstone modestly read: 'stone carver'.

A versatile figure emerging out of the arts and crafts movement, Gill's 11 typeface designs remain a seminal influence. Even today, most have been digitised and Perpetua and Gill Sans Serif, in particular, remain cornerstones of British typeface design history.

El Lissitzky

El (Lazar Markovich) Lissitzky was a leader in the Russian constructivist movement, working as a teacher, architect, poster and book designer, as well as an exhibition designer.

Born 1890, Pochinok, Russia
Importance Influential intermediary of the graphic revolution
Died 1941, Moscow, USSR

His use of simple, geometric forms and innovative ways with photography and photomontage made him one of the key figures in the revolution that was taking place in the graphic arts.

In addition to his work, El Lissitzky was an important propagandist and personality who frequently travelled between Russia and the rest of Western Europe, particularly Germany, Switzerland and the Netherlands. This gave him a tremendously important role as a conduit and intermediary between constructivism (see page 40) and the modernist New Typographers (see page 108) working simultaneously across Europe in the 1920s. Like his colleagues in the constructivist movement – Alexander Rodchenko, Gustav Klutsis, the Stenberg Brothers and Vladimir Tatlin – El Lissitzky felt 'art' must take a new and practical role in the development and betterment of society. Thus they often turned their attention to printed material and propaganda. Science and technology must also play a crucial role, and the constructivists called for the dismissal of the old bourgeois techniques of illustration and painting in favour of the mechanical.

Trained as an architect at the Polytechnische Hochschule in Darmstadt, Germany, El Lissitzky applied many of the tools of engineering and architecture to his graphic works. His self-portrait collage entitled *Constructor* (1924) perhaps best sums up the revolutionary shift that was taking place in the graphic arts: he portrayed himself using photomontage, his large hand holding a compass – a tool of the engineer. The whole image appeared to be composed on a piece of graph paper. Even the lettering was not hand drawn, but taken from a stencil. The constructivists, like their political leader Vladimir Lenin, understood that, for the Bolshevik Revolution to be successful, Russia must industrialise itself quickly. El Lissitzky, in fact, often used actual parts of the printing press (leading, kerning) to create his forms.

Most influential for El Lissitzky were the works of his close friend Kasimir Malevich, whose suprematist paintings hoped to reduce painting to 'its supreme emotional expression'. By simplifying a work to areas of colour on white canvas, Malevich created canvases that were about a physical, retinal experience. In El Lissitzky's most important work, the 1919 *Beat the Whites with the Red Wedge*, he used pure abstraction for the first time in graphics, believing that 'concepts should be expressed with the greatest economy'. A similar use of abstraction occurs in his book of Vladimir Mayakosky's poems *To be read out loud* and in the story *About 2 squares*, intended for children. In all these examples abstract forms are used to deliver the narrative.

In no other historical period does the field of graphic design take on such a significant role sanctioned by the state. Additionally, no other period offers the kind of intellectual vigour that was attached to the profession during this time. In 1933, Stalin proclaimed 'Social Realism' the official style of the state and for use in all propaganda, thus putting an end to this truly remarkable period. Nonetheless the innovations that took place during these short 10 to 15 years – in what had been a relative backwater – were astounding.

El Lissitzky's Beat the Whites with the Red Wedge *(1919).*

Laszlo Moholy-Nagy

Although an early pioneer of Russian constructivism and Dada avant-garde, Laszlo Moholy-Nagy is best known as having been a key promoter and figurehead of the German Bauhaus school and design philosophy.

Born 1895, Borsod, Hungary
Importance Avant-garde Hungarian Dada- and Constructivist-influenced artist, leading figure of the Bauhaus school and movement
Died 1946, Chicago, Illinois, United States

Born Laszlo Weisz, in Borsod, (now Bácsborsód) in Hungary, Moholy-Nagy entered the University of Budapest in 1913 to study law. He enlisted in the Austro-Hungarian army in 1915, and by the time he was injured on the Russian front in 1917 (his left thumb was mutilated by shrapnel), he had created over 400 drawings on army issue postcards. When he was discharged from the army at the end of the war, Weisz abandoned his law studies to become an artist. He took life-drawing evening classes at Robert Berény's art school in Budapest and developed a keen interest in the works of the Russian avant-gardists and German expressionists.

In 1920, he moved to Berlin, where he met German Dada artists. By this time he had changed his German-Jewish surname Weisz to his uncle's surname, Nagy. Later, he would preface Nagy with Moholy, taken from the town in which he grew up. That same year, Moholy-Nagy began to work on collages, which exhibited the first signs of a Russian constructivist influence. In tandem, he published *Horizont*, a collection of his Dada-inspired artworks.

Moholy-Nagy soon caught the attention of Bauhaus founder Walter Gropius with his Telephone Paintings, five machine-made paintings featuring enamel on steel, complete with numbers and letters, as if product codes issued by the factory. In 1923, he was invited to Weimar to lecture at the newly-founded Staatliche Bauhaus school, where he began teaching foundation courses and oversaw the metal workshop. He made a decisive move away from teaching the 'spiritual values' that had been so prevalent at the Bauhaus to date, and instead focused on the mechanics and logics of form. He taught his students the nature and composition of different materials – Plexiglass and steel were key. He also placed enormous emphasis on the tools that students employed, urging them to use compasses and rulers over any hand-drawn work, all the while embracing the Bauhaus ideals of production and technology.

Composition # 19 *(1928):*
a typically geometric design.

By 1925, Moholy-Nagy was a hugely instrumental figure at the Bauhaus school and moved to the new Dessau campus. He and Gropius began to develop a book-publishing programme, dedicated to documenting and disseminating Bauhaus principles. Moholy-Nagy introduced a bold sans-serif type, which he used not only for headings and sub-headings, but also for single words that he wanted to draw attention to. He insisted that typographic design should reflect content.

He left the Bauhaus school in 1928 and moved back to Berlin, where he worked as an artist and remained active in the Bauhaus publishing programme. By 1930, they had published 14 books, 11 of which were designed by Moholy-Nagy. He also wrote the eighth book in the series, *Painting Photography Film.*

In 1939, Moholy-Nagy and colleagues opened The School of Design in Chicago, known today as the Institute of Design of the Illinois Institute of Technology.

A cross-disciplinary artist in the most real sense of the term, Moholy-Nagy's groundbreaking work and philosophies continue to resonate and have had a deep-rooted impact on design history.

BAUHAUS

During the 1920s, the Bauhaus school in Germany became the epicentre of what was to mark a radical shift in graphic design thinking, moving away from expressionist leanings and, instead, bridging the gap between the mechanics and the aesthetics of art, all the while championing the idea that graphic design must, above anything else, be functional.

T he Bauhaus School of Arts and Crafts was founded in Weimar, Germany, in January 1919 by German architect Walter Gropius. For 14 years, the school pioneered new artistic pathways, combined fine arts with design education and exacted a radical influence in all areas of design. At the time of the school's launch, Germany was stricken with inflation, political instability and unemployment in the aftermath of the First World War.

From its founding until 1922, the school's ideological development was shaped by Johannes Itten, who taught the preliminary course introducing the ideas of Bauhaus. Other key faculty members included artists Paul Klee and Wassily Kandinsky, and visiting lecturer El Lissitzky (who brought a Russian constructivist influence). The school was mostly driven by Itten's preoccupation with German expressionism which fed into the overall aesthetic and ethos during this time.

In 1923, Laszlo Moholy-Nagy joined the school and helped pioneer what is today considered archetypal Bauhaus typography. Characteristics of the style included the use

'In restricting ourselves to lower-case letters, our type loses nothing, but becomes more easily read, more easily learned, substantially more economic.'

Herbert Bayer

of rules, sans-serif typefaces and lower case. The Bauhaus started to move towards what was called a 'machine aesthetic', drawing heavily on influences from the De Stijl and Russian constructivist movements. Moholy-Nagy arrived at the school just as Itten was leaving and very quickly began to assume control of the curriculum. He wanted to move away from 'spritual values' in design and to work towards ideals revolving around function and form instead. Many consider this shift to be about changing the perception of the artist to that of an engineer.

Of the school's in-house typographic style, Moholy-Nagy said, 'We all use typefaces, type sizes, geometric forms, colours, etc'. In 1926, Herbert Bayer, who had become director of printing and publicity at the school, visualised Moholy-Nagy's comment perfectly, when he designed a new typeface for school communications: Universal.

The school created various Bauhaus publications over the years, all of which have had a lasting influence on graphic design. Arguably the most significant was the catalogue for the 1923 exhibition 'Staatliches Bauhaus im Weimar 1919–1923'. The catalogue was designed by Moholy-Nagy and the binding by Herbert Bayer. The format was square, with the text hanging from the square grid layout. This was a pivotal point in the growth of Bauhaus's visual language.

By 1929, Moholo-Nagy recorded his thoughts on how typography and photography were able to collaborate as a style he called 'typo-foto'. In his Bauhaus publication *Malerei, Fotografie, Film* (*Painting, Photography, Film*), he offered various contemplations of this new form: 'typography is communication composed in type', 'photography is the visual presentation of what can be optically apprehended' and 'typo-foto is the visually most exact rendering of communication.' Moholy-Nagy continued to promote a functionalist aesthetic, telling students that, 'To be a user of machines is to be of the spirit of this century. It has replaced the transcendent spiritualism of past eras.'

In 1933, the Bauhaus school was closed by the Nazis, who accused the faculty and students of 'cultural Bolshevism'. Many founding members fled to the United States, including Moholy-Nagy.

Herbert Bayer

Herbert Bayer, like Laszlo Moholy-Nagy and Walter Gropius, accomplished much across his lifetime of work, yet remains best-celebrated for his contributions to the Bauhaus movement and role within the school throughout the 1920s.

Born 1900, Haag, Austria
Importance Key figure of the Bauhaus school and designer of the Universal typeface
Died 1985, Montecito, California, United States

Born in a small village near Salzburg, Austria, Herbert Bayer began his career in 1919 with an apprenticeship alongside architect and designer Georg Schmidthamer in Linz. During this time, he designed letterheads, posters and advertisements and developed a keen eye for typography. In 1921, he moved to Darmstadt in Germany, where he worked for architect Emmanuel Margold at the Darmstadt Artists Colony. Exposed to art nouveau influences, he was heavily influenced by Walter Gropius's book *Bauhaus Manifesto*.

Bayer applied to study at the Bauhaus school and, after impressing Gropius, was accepted into a trial pre-studies workshop, studying mural painting alongside the artist Wassily Kandinsky. He was then accepted into the school as a full-time student. When Bayer graduated in 1925, Gropius was in the process of moving the school from Weimar to Dessau and invited Bayer to head up the new printing and advertising workshop.

Bayer became active in the branding and identity of the newly relocated school. In October 1925, he brought in the lower-case alphabet as the in-school house standard for all Bauhaus printed materials. Asked by Gropius to design a new Bauhaus typeface to accompany the lower-case creed, Bayer conceived an 'idealist typeface' which he called Universal. The principle theory behind its design was to create a singular, all-encompassing 'world style' that could be translated across all different variations, which at the time Bayer

translated across all different variations, which at the time Bayer identified as handwritten, typewritten (or typeset) and printed. While such theories were hugely optimistic, the implications were to encourage a standardised typeface that did away with any sense of individuality. As such, the somewhat geometric sans-serif font became perfectly emblematic of the Bauhaus ethos. Turning his vision to the identity of the campus itself, Bayer designed a signage system for the Dessau site.

In 1928, he broke from Bauhaus and moved to Berlin, where he concentrated on his work as an artist while finding commercial success working as a designer. He undertook design work within advertising, notably for advertising agency Studio Dorland. Bayer also became art director for Paris *Vogue* during the 1930s.

In 1938, he moved to the United States. Once there, he helped to introduce the Bauhaus teachings in the form of the exhibition 'Bauhaus 1919–1928', held at MoMA. The exhibition and its catalogue documented the key achievements of the Bauhaus and remain an iconic presentation of the school, which closed under Nazi pressure in 1933.

In 1946, Bayer settled in Aspen, Colorado, where he worked as a graphic designer, architect, painter, landscape designer and photographer – continuing to create a life's work that embraced multiple disciplines.

By the time he died in California, at the age of 85, he had achieved much as an artist, yet his pioneering work during the 1920s as part of the Bauhaus school remains the zenith of his legacy. His use of the lower-case alphabet remains influential across all spectrums of graphic design.

Herbert Bayer visiting the 'Modern Art in Advertising' exhibition in 1941.

Jan Tschichold

Jan Tschichold was one of the most outstanding and influential typographers of the twentieth century. He blazed a trail under the influence of the Bauhaus style as a typeface designer, typographer and author, in all cases helping to bring typography into the modern age.

Born 1902, Leipzig, Germany

Importance
Celebrated twentieth-century typographer, writer and book designer

Died 1974, Locarno, Switzerland

Tschichold was born in Leipzig. Influenced by a visit to the World's Fair for Books and Graphics in 1914, Tschichold found inspiration in Edward Johnston's *Calligraphy, Ornamental Script and Applied Script* and *Study in Ornamental Writing* by Rudolf Von Larisch, and he began to experiment with forms of calligraphy. In 1917, he entered the Academy for Graphic Arts in Leipzig, determined to become a typeface designer. There, he studied typography under Hermann Delitsch, as well as bookbinding, woodcutting, engraving and wood engraving. In the early 1920s, he incorporated his calligraphy skills into poster designs and spent much time studying the form and composition of typefaces, influenced by the work of German author, designer and calligrapher Rudolf Koch. In 1923, he became a type designer for Fischer & Wittig, a book printer.

Sample type in Tschichold's 1931 font Saskia.

After visiting the first Bauhaus exhibition in 1924, Tschichold fell under the spell of Laszlo Moholy-Nagy and El Lissitzky. He revealed his new Bauhaus-inspired approach to typography in his article, 'Elementary Typography', published in the October 1925 issue of *Typographic News*. In his pseudo-manifesto, he championed Bauhaus ideas: typography must prioritise communication and function; only sans-serif typefaces must be used; and photography offers the simplest image. Some applauded his vision, though most criticised it.

Tschichold moved to Munich, where he taught at the Master School for Germany's Printers, founded by Paul Renner. There, he taught typography and calligraphy while maintaining his own practice and developing his writing – in 1928, he published his first seminal instructional book, *The New Typography*. The book suggested a uniform, standardised approach to typography and page composition.

Continuing to work under the influence of the Bauhaus style, Tschichold moved into typeface design, designing Transit, Saskia and Zeus, all in 1931. Soon after, his work fell under criticism from the Nazis, who forbade him from teaching or practising as a designer. Forced to flee to Switzerland, he taught at the Basel School of Applied Arts and worked as a book designer for Birkäuser publishing.

In 1946, Tschichold moved to London to work as typographer for Penguin Books. While there, Tschichold designed and wrote a set of typographic rules that came to be known as the *Penguin Composition Rules*. The four-page essay explained why designers needed to follow his standardised recommendations regarding layout and typography. He struck a perfect balance between creating an overarching look for the books, while still allowing each book (and its content) to be reflected in the design.

Moving back to Switzerland at the end of the 1940s, he published another classic book, *The Master Book of Typefaces*. In 1955, Tschichold joined Hoffman-La Roche, a firm based in Basel, Switzerland, as a typographer and worked there until 1967. The remaining years of his life were devoted to designing and lecturing. His pioneering modern representations of type ushered in the new Bauhaus-inspired approach.

NEW TYPOGRAPHY

The New Typography movement was spearheaded by Laszlo Moholy-Nagy and typographer Jan Tschichold in the mid-1920s. It called into question many of the conventions associated with typography and asked for a very different approach to the role of typography within visual communication.

The roots of New Typography hark back to the early years of the Bauhaus school, which was founded in 1919 (see page 102). The school's graphic design department had evolved a Bauhaus style, which meant a preference for sans-serif typefaces typified by Herbert Bayer's Universal (1923) and Josef Albers's Stencil (1925). Bauhaus typographers took a particular interest in the way that the impersonal character of sans-serif typefaces worked harmoniously and discretely with the photographic image. Other Bauhaus typographic traits included the common use of rules (strips of wood or metal that printed as solid lines), a technique used to create a new emblem for the school in 1924: a geometrical profile of a human face.

In 1923, at a Bauhaus exhibition in Weimar, calligrapher, typographer and professor Jan Tschichold was struck by the work displayed by Moholy-Nagy, and in particular, by his use of the phrase 'New Typography' in an essay he had written for the exhibition catalogue. After that, Tschichold associated himself with Moholy-Nagy and the Russian constructivist artist and designer El Lissitzky, and joined the crusade to transform the future of typography.

Two years later, Tschichold announced his ideas by editing *Elementare Typographie* (*Elementary Typography*), a special edition of *Typographische Mitteilunger* (*Typographic News*). Intended to showcase the latest Bauhaus creations, the anthology of writings also featured El Lissitzky and Kurt Schwitters. The work was all arguably overshadowed by Tschichold's manifesto of sorts, calling for a 'New Typography'.

His key ideas included the following: 'typography is shaped by functional requirements'; 'the aim of typographic layout is communication (for which it is the graphic medium)'; 'communication must appear in the shortest, simplest, most penetrating form'; 'for typography to serve social ends, its ingredients need internal organisation (ordered content), as well as external organisation (the typographic material properly related)'.

> *'Words on the printed sheet are seen, not heard.'*
>
> El Lissitzky

Tschichold went on to argue in favour of photography, sans-serif typefaces, bold rules, asymmetry and the importance of negative space as a positive contrast. He also argued against all decorative elements except the use of the triangle, square and circle (all three of which were also recurring motifs in Russian constructivist work, see page 40). The cover of the special edition was a synthesis of Tschichold's ideas, featuring only red and black and two geometric lines, set against an off-white background of empty space. The entire text was also set in lower case.

Sharing Tschichold's interest in New Typography was Kurt Schwitters, who launched his own journal, *Merz*, in 1923. The fourth issue included El Lissitzky's *Topography of Typography*, a list of seven themes for a New Typography. Schwitters himself pushed typography in *Merz*, devotedly using only sans-serif typefaces and heavy rules dividing pages to powerful visual effect.

Herbert Bayer played a significant role in popularising New Typography as director of the Bauhaus printing and publicity department, a role that saw him oversee the creation of much of the Bauhaus printed matter, all adhering to the Bauhaus style.

In 1928, Tschichold documented his typographical invention in the seminal graphic design book, *The New Typography*. However, the movement was soon to disintegrate, in 1933, when the Nazis closed the Bauhaus school, pronouncing their ideology 'cultural Bolshevism', and sending key figures, such as Tschichold and Schwitters, into exile.

Hermann Zapf

Typeface designer, book designer and calligrapher Hermann Zapf has designed 200 typefaces in his lifetime, several of which – Palatino, Optima, Zapf Dingbats and Zapfino – are all standard systems fonts.

Born 1918, Nuremberg, Germany
Importance Seminal self-taught typeface designer of Palatino, Optima and Zapfino typefaces

Zapf began his career at just 16 years old with an apprenticeship at printers Karl Ulrich & Co in Hamburg. He had wanted to study electrical engineering, but because of his father's trade union affiliations he was blacklisted both from education and employment by the rising Nazi party. According to myth, encouraged by an art teacher to become a lithographer, Zapf tried to find an apprenticeship with every printing company listed in the telephone directory – and it wasn't until the listings for U that he received a response from Karl Ulrich & Co, who offered to train him as a retoucher.

In 1935, Zapf attended an exhibition featuring work by Rudolf Koch, and was inspired. He bought exhibition catalogues by Edward Johnston and Koch, and used them to teach himself calligraphy. Four years later, he finished his apprenticeship and began working at the Frankfurt printing workshop Werkstatt Haus zum Fürsteneck, learning fine printing arts, such as hand-press lettering and punch cutting.

A 1963 exhibition poster showcases Zapf's many styles of typography.

Zapf's career was interrupted by the Second World War, during which he worked as an army cartographer in France. After the war, he taught calligraphy in Nuremburg before joining the Stempel AG type foundry, for whom he had briefly worked before the war as artistic director. There, he began a period of tremendous creativity, designing a range of fonts that serve as standards today: the highly legible serif typeface, Palatino (1948); Optima, a humanist sans-serif typeface whose elegant strokes were inspired by calligraphy (1958); and Sistina, an antiquated typeface based on Roman inscriptions, and initially released in capitals (1951). Simultaneously, he taught calligraphy at the Arts and Crafts School in Offenbach. Alongside both, he worked as a graphic artist, specialising in book design for German publishing houses.

PUNCH CUTTING
Punch cutting is the traditional craft of cutting letter punches in steel, which can then be used to make matrices in copper. The process helps to facilitate typesetting.

In 1957, Zapf became an advisor to the New York-based Linotype Company, a role that lasted until 1974. He also began teaching typography at the Technische Hochschule in Darmstadt from 1972 until 1981. At the same time, he was appointed Professor of Typographic Computer Programming at the Rochester Institute of Technology in New York in 1977, where, for the next decade, he played a pioneering role in helping digitise fonts to facilitate computer-aided typesetting.

Zapf continued typeface design, creating the ITC Zapf Book typeface in 1976, which branched off into the ITC Zapf Dingbats typeface a year later – some 360 signs and symbols of Zapf's creation. ITC Zapf Chancery followed in 1979. In 1982, Zapf's work was honoured in the United States when Optima was chosen as the typeface for the Memorial Wall at the Vietnam Veteran's Memorial in Washington DC.

Ever since, Zapf has been dedicated to educating and creating, continuously adapting his expertise to the latest technological developments, while devising yet more brilliant typefaces, including Zapfino, at the aged of 81. He remains a seminal figure for his role in the transition from hand typesetting to the digitised computer era.

Herb Lubalin

After learning his trade in New York advertising, Herb Lubalin launched his own studio and impressed many with his provocative, expressive approach to typography. He is best remembered for having launched the magazine *U&lc*, which many have said paved the way for *Emigré* magazine.

Born 1918, New York City, New York, United States
Importance Innovative American typographer known for his expressive, communicative approach to design.
Died 1981, New York City, New York, United States

At the age of 17, Lubalin went to study at Cooper Union and graduated in 1939 with a passion for typography and its potential as a means of communication. He worked at Reiss Advertising in the 1940s, before moving to another advertising agency, Sudler & Hennessey, this time for a two-decade-long stint.

In 1952, Lubalin won industry recognition in the guise of a New York Art Directors Club Gold Medal for his work as creative director at Sudler & Hennessey. Arguably, his most significant work began in 1964, when he left to launch his own design consultancy firm, Herb Lubalin, Inc, which became a hub for associate talent. In 1969, the firm renamed itself, LSC, Inc and later, in 1975, LSC&P Design Group.

During this time, Lublin's typographic vision, gradually began to move away from the Bauhaus and Swiss Style emphasis on functionality (see pages 102 and 32), and instead favoured an expressive, almost emotive focus. He rejected the minimalist, white-space creed of the Swiss Style and Bauhaus in favour of powerful and bold designs. This goes some way to explaining why Lubalin's designs have often been compared to the emerging chaotic rock 'n' roll sound of the time. It was a shift best seen in a cluster of magazines, *Eros*, *Fact* and *Avant Garde*, all founded by Ralph Ginzburg, and each of which bore Lubalin's typefaces.

Aa Bb Cc Dd
Ee Ff Gg Hh

Lubalin's font Avant Garde (1970) is characterised by its rounded letters.

Eros launched in 1962 and was a risqué hardcover 'magbook' quarterly, dedicated to covering anything to do with love and sex. Its content attracted much controversy, and obscenity charges against the publisher led to its folding after four issues. In 1964, Ginzburg and Lubalin partnered again with the political journal *Fact*, which Lubalin designed with a discrete minimalist approach. The second title also folded prematurely three years after its launch, following litigation.

Their third magazine, *Avant Garde*, devoted to coverage of the arts and culture, launched in 1968. Here, Lubalin's typographic inventiveness and innovative layouts shone. His logo for the magazine alone was seen as the very embodiment of the moment. Using evenly weighted letters – all capitals – Lubalin added sharp, angled stems on the A and the V of 'Avant'. Once the logo concept was complete, Lubalin and his studio partner, Tom Carnase, adapated it as a typeface, and in 1970, ITC released the Avant Garde fonts commercially. The magazine pushed boundaries graphically – one cover featured a naked, pregnant model. Despite its admirers, *Avant Garde* was also short-lived, and folded in 1971.

In 1973, Lubalin founded *U&lc* (shorthand for 'Upper and lower case'), a typographic journal that paved the way for similarly-focused *Emigré* magazine. The last eight years of Lubalin's life were filled with overseeing *U&lc* and launching International Typographic Corporation, a new expanded department within his consultancy. He remains celebrated for his loud and expressive 1960s typographic work.

Armin Hofmann

Armin Hofmann was a seminal figure in the Swiss Style graphic design movement. Working as a designer, author and educator, he is best known for his poster designs, which typically favour simplicity expressed through a minimalist use of fonts – often black and white – in order to challenge what he would boldly call the 'trivialisation of colour'.

Born 1920, Winterthur, Switzerland
Importance Major figure in the popularisation of the Swiss Style

Having undertaken a lithography apprenticeship, Hofmann came to prominence in 1947 when he began teaching at the Basel School of Design, a loose umbrella that brought together designers Emil Ruder, Armin Hofmann, Burkhard Mangold, Niklaus Stoecklin, Herbert Leupin and Wolfgang Weingart. Hofmann's involvement there would last nearly four decades, with him leaving the school in 1986. There, along with Emil Ruder, Hofmann actively promoted the typographic ideals of the Swiss Style (see page 32).

Together, they introduced what they called the school's typographic principles, whose characteristics were generally defined by design critic Steven Heller as follows: 'A correct balance between form and function, the sanctity of readability and the belief in an absolute and universal graphic expression.' This ethos became the epicentre of teaching practice at the Basel School of Design.

During his lengthy tenure, Hofmann designed many classic posters. His 1960 poster *Art Education in the USA* typifies his style: at once stark and functional, the poster was made up of a white illustration of an eye sitting against a black background. The type, which was also white, was functional. A 1964 poster of a Rothko exhibit in Basel featured bold black type and a background that borrowed an autumnal red and maroon from Rothko's own

Hofmann's posters frequently made use of strong monotone type.

trademark palette. Both works espouse all the typographic principles that Hofmann championed at the Basel school.

In 1965, Hofmann published his *Graphic Design Manual*, outlining the discipline's basic principles. Now widely acclaimed, the work became a seminal textbook and has since had a profound impact on decades of design education. Since his retirement in 1987, Hofmann remains the primary educator of the Swiss Style, his vision for design proving hugely influential to this day.

Adrian Frutiger

Acclaimed for his innovative and prolific typeface design, Adrian Frutiger is most celebrated for creating Univers, Meridien and Frutiger. He has also proved a keen advocate of new technological developments in the printing process, and has written a number of successful books on the subject of typography.

Born 1928, Unterseen, Switzerland
Importance Prolific typeface designer, most notable for Frutiger and Univers

As a child, Frutiger developed a passion for calligraphy, famously cutting his pen down to a broad nib at school in order to make sure his letterforms were rounded and expansive. This led him to an apprenticeship as a compositor for printer Otto Schaerffli in his hometown of Interlaken, Switzerland.

An avid reader of the Swiss typography magazine *Typografische Monatsblätter*, Frutiger learned a great deal about the Basel School of Design through its pages. Upon completing his apprenticeship, he moved to Zurich to study at the Kunstgewerbeschule (Zurich School of Arts and Crafts) from 1949 to 1951. While in Zurich, he sought out Emil Ruder, a professor at the Basel School of Design, and thoroughly impressed him with one of his typographic woodcuts.

In 1951, Frutiger moved to Paris to work for the Deberny & Peignot foundry. It was there that he put his training into practice, designing new typefaces and encouraging the foundry to embrace new phototypesetting technology. As his experience grew, he began to design his own typefaces. The first, President, was released in 1952. Phoebus (1953) and Ondine (1954) followed. Then came the first of his typefaces to maintain classical status today, Méridien (1955). A year later came Egyptienne and then his outright classic: the sans-serif Univers (French for universe), which Deberny & Peignot released in 1957. The typeface is renowned for its high degree of legibility at long distances, and has been used by international companies such as Apple Inc, General Electric, Swiss International Air Lines and Deutsche Bank, and institutions such as Frankfurt international airport. Today Univers is available in 27 different versions.

In 1961, Frutiger left the foundry and opened his own studio in the suburbs of Paris, in partnership with Bruno Pfäffli and André Gürtler. His studio was successful and won clients such as IBM and the Stempel foundry. In 1962, the studio designed the Apollo typeface; Serifa in 1967; OCR-B in 1968; and both Iridium and Frutiger in 1975.

The story behind typeface Frutiger began in 1968, when Frutiger's studio won a commission to design a signage system for Roissy airport in Paris (later Charles de Gaulle airport). Frutiger opted for a bold font to increase legibility, making sure the letterforms were clear in poor weather conditions and obvious to passers-by in a hurry. His plans were implemented across the airport in 1975, and his specially designed typeface, originally called Roissy, was later renamed Frutiger.

From 1980 onwards, Frutiger wrote a number of books, including *Type, Sign, Symbol* (1980), *Signs and Symbols: Their Design and Meaning* (1989), *The International Type Book* (1990), *Geometry of Feelings* (1998) and *Symbols and Signs: Explorations* (1999).

In 2008, Frutiger created a new version of Meridien, to celebrate his 80th birthday. Linotype commercially released the typeface as Frutiger Serif. His legacy remains that of a pioneering typeface designer. As well as designing iconic typefaces that continue to be used today, Frutiger also played a key role in seeing classic typefaces adapted to new printing methods.

Renowned typographer Adrien Frutiger at work.

Matthew Carter

Trained in the traditional methods of type design and letterforms, Carter skilfully created typefaces that combined old-school conventions with the very latest printing technologies. It is very much because of this skill that Carter's designs have tremendous relevance to the field of graphic design today.

Born 1937, London, England
Importance Brilliantly married the conventions of old-school typesetting with the latest developing technology

The son of English typographer, type historian and book designer, Harry Carter, Matthew Carter was exposed to the power and potential of type throughout his childhood. Having won a place to study at English literature at Oxford University, yet unable to start for a year, Carter took up an internship at Johannes Enschede en Zonen, a printer and type founder in Haarlem, the Netherlands. There he studied punch cutting and became so immersed in the craft that he never enrolled at Oxford University, but worked on various projects for his father instead.

Carter was trained in the setting of metal type by hand, which taught him the most intricate methods of working with type. The expertise required in placing a letter, knowing the form it took, judging the space between two letters, and so on, trained Carter in the minutiae of the old-school craft. With the progress of technology, Carter was able to marry the two: his knowledge of the traditional printing process with the advance of photosetting technologies and, later, digitised type, adapting his training with tremendous skill.

By 1960, Carter was working as a freelance type designer in London, which he did for the next 20 years, except for a brief spell (1965–1971) working as in-house type designer for Mergenthaler Linotype in New York. It was here that he designed typefaces suited to the new photosetting technologies, such as Snell Roundhand (1966).

Aa Bb Cc Dd
Ee Ff Gg Hh

Sans-serif font Verdana was specifically created for ease of on-screen reading.

Leaving New York for London in 1971 and freelance again, Carter worked primarily for Linotype companies, but also for corporate giants such as AT&T, who set him a brief to redesign their telephone directories in 1974. Carter's response was Bell Centennial, which became the standard issue in the company's telephone directories in 1978. This acclaimed typeface won Carter international attention.

In 1977, Carter became the senior critic for Yale University's graphic design master of fine arts (MFA) programme, a position he has held ever since. In 1980, his reputation earned him a four-year role as typographical advisor to Her Majesty's Stationery Office in the UK.

In 1981, Carter co-founded the digital type foundry, Bitstream, Inc in the US, with Cherie Cone, Rob Friedman and Mike Parker. The digital type library caught the moment, with the booming desktop publishing, digital production and the PC markets. In 1991, Carter and Cherie Cone left Bitstream, Inc to found Carter & Cone Type, Inc, also based in the US and still active today.

Throughout the 1990s, Carter continued to work as a successful type designer, creating Wrigly for *Sports Illustrated*; Sophia for the Museum of Fine Arts, Boston; Bodoni for the *Washington Post*; Walbaum for *Wired* magazine; and Walker for the Walker Arts Centre in Minneapolis. His highest profile typeface to date remains Verdana, a humanist sans-serif typeface which was created in 1996 for Microsoft's standard operation systems and Internet Explorer.

Today, Carter remains as active as ever and his iconic typeface designs for Microsoft and AT&T continue to be used and seen by millions of people every day.

Ed Fella

Artist, designer and educator Ed Fella is thought to have had two lives: the first as a commercial artist in Detroit, and the second as an educator, mostly producing self-initiated work exploring hand-drawn typography and Polaroids capturing the American vernacular.

Born 1938, Detroit, Michigan, United States
Importance Artist, educator and graphic designer whose work has had an important influence on contemporary typography and the notion of the vernacular

Fella worked as a commercial artist until the age of 47, when he enrolled to study fine arts at the Cranbrook Academy of Art. Thereafter, he blurred the fine art/graphic design boundary, creating a rich body of work that has often been praised for breaking all the fundamental rules of graphic design.

Fella studied the craft of commercial art, including illustration, paste-up and lettering, at Cass Technical High School in his hometown of Detroit, Michigan. He was struck by classes on Bauhaus methodology (see page 102) – in particular the Bauhaus belief in erasing boundaries between applied and fine art. He graduated in 1957 and found work as an apprentice at a studio offering services to the city's advertising industry. From there, he moved to working as a full-time commercial artist, later freelancing predominantly for healthcare and car industry clients.

Throughout the 1960s, Fella kept a studio where, in his spare time, he painted large-scale abstract paintings. To offset the tedium of many projects, he undertook much self-initiated work, experimenting with typefaces, photocopiers, collage and hand-drawn lettering.

Fella credits his meeting with Katharine McCoy and Lorraine Wild at the advertising art studio Designers and Partners in Detroit, in the early 1970s, with his eventual track towards becoming an 'exit-level designer', an oft-cited self-description. McCoy left Designers and Partners to become head of the design department at Cranbrook

Academy of Art. She regularly invited Fella to present his work to her students. Meanwhile, Fella made associations with arts organisations in Detroit and began to find an outlet for his personal work. During the course of the 1970s and 1980s, scores of vivid posters and related printed materials, appeared across Detroit's arts scene, all bearing Fella's battered, rugged approach, his trademark aesthetic.

In the early 1980s, Fella pursued his

This 1990s promotional card demonstrates Fella's colourful, hand-drawn typography.

undergraduate studies at the Center for Creative Studies in Detroit and in 1985, aged 47, he enrolled in Cranbrook's master of fine arts design programme, in order to gain the necessary academic qualifications and validate his typographic experimentation. It was here that his artistic side flourished, solidifying his belief in 'graphic design as art'. His sketchbooks and notebooks and ephemera collections have since become legendary. He graduated in 1987 and was hired by old Detroit associate and fellow Cranbrook alumna, Lorraine Wild, to teach at CalArts. On accepting the lecturing post, Fella retired from commercial work and devoted himself to academia and self-initiated work. In 2000, Princeton Architectural Press published Fella's monograph, *Letters on America*. Probably the best example of Fella's self-initiated work, the book is a collection of Fella's polaroids capturing American vernacular typography in all its glory, interspersed with his hand-drawn lettering experiments. At once playful, messy and beautifully composed, they encapsulate Fella's sense of anti-mastery.

Wolfgang Weingart

Typographer, author and educator Wolfgang Weingart, began as a student of the Swiss Style, before reinventing the movement with ideas of his own, which resulted in the New Wave approach to typography. His innovative design did much to undo the tidiness of the Swiss Style, and paved the way for future innovators such as April Greiman and David Carson.

Born 1941, Konstanz, Germany
Importance
Responsible for the New Wave typography that dominated the postmodern era

As a young boy, Weingart famously dismantled his bicycle and learned how to reassemble it, launching a lifetime's fascination with the mechanical composition of things. In 1958, he undertook a three-year apprenticeship in hand composition with a typesetter. There, he often questioned and challenged the process, for example, he once designed a set of curved rules, instead of traditional straight ones, which enabled him to craft a series of letterpress prints.

When he completed the apprenticeship, he moved from Germany to Switzerland, to study at the Basel School of Design under Armin Hofmann and Emil Ruder, two strong voices of the Swiss Style (see page 32). In 1968, Hofmann, impressed by Weingart's energetic work and ideas, offered him a position teaching typography.

Weingart later wrote in *Design Quarterly* about teaching during a time when the Swiss Style was the only approach the Basel school adhered to, saying: 'Its conservative design dogma and strict limitations stifled my playful, inquisitive, experimental temperament and I reacted strongly against it. Yet at the same time I recognised too many good qualities in Swiss typography to renounce it altogether. Through my teaching I set out to use the positive qualities of Swiss typography as a base from which to pursue radically new typographic frontiers.' Grafting his own ideas onto Hofmann's Swiss Style template, Weingart arrived at what became known as New Wave typography (see page 124) or the 'Swiss punk' style. Key elements of this new style included: deviating from the strict adherence to grid-based design; abandoning the traditional paragraph indentations; inconsistent letter spacing; setting type at irregular angles; changing type weight within a single word; and placing emphasis on any one word within a headline. The results were anarchic, rugged, rough, confrontational and a definitive move away from the Swiss Style.

Weingart challenged various conventions. He saw no value to legibility if it did not generate an effect – if nobody looked, the design had failed. He held onto the idea of simplicity though, famously telling students that only four typefaces are required to address all forms and kinds of typographic problems. At the Basel school, Weingart introduced these new ideas to eager students, including April Greiman, who practised Weingart's New Wave typography on her return to the United States.

Weingart went on to found the journals *Typographic Process* and *TM/Communication*, as well as writing for many titles and teaching and lecturing internationally, with CalArts, Yale, Princeton and the Cooper Hewitt Museum among his regular venues. In 2000, Weingart brought his career-long ideas together in the book *My Way to Typography*. The book took five years to create and offers the best insights into one of the most inquisitive minds of graphic design history.

A Weingart-designed poster for the Kunst Gewerbe Museum.

NEW WAVE

Emerging out of, and in response to, the Swiss Style, the New Wave was spearheaded by German designer, Wolfgang Weingart. It turned the formal rules of the Swiss Style upside down to arrive at a new, dynamic approach to design in the late 1960s and 1970s. This new, radical approach, popularised by Weingart in Europe, was then introduced in the United States by April Greiman (and by Weingart through his regular visits to Cranbrook Academy of Art in Michigan).

The journey towards New Wave started when Weingart arrived in Switzerland to study at the Basel School of Design under Emil Ruder and Armin Hofmann – both keen advocates of the Swiss Style (see page 32). Graduating in 1968, Weingart began teaching typography and started to challenge his Swiss Style training.

His new style was known as New Wave typography or 'Swiss punk'. It was a rugged and confrontational style where legibility was not considered a crucial criterion. Instead, Weingart looked to deconstruct the accepted Swiss Style and its adherence to a regular grid system that relied on consistent letter spacing and weight. New Wave focused on geometric forms, bright colours and irregular letter angles, and also deviated from traditional

'I took "Swiss Typography" as my starting point, but then I blew it apart, never forcing any style upon my students. I never intended to create a "style". It just happened that the students picked up – and misinterpreted – a so-called "Weingart style" and spread it around.'

Wolfgang Weingart

rules, such as paragraph indentation. The style was less about readability and more about the importance of good design being able to demand attention.

In the early 1970s, a young American student, April Greiman, came to Basel to study under Weingart and graduated inspired by his visions for New Wave. She returned to the United States and, through her own design practice Made In Space Inc, popularised Weingart's New Wave approach. Her own unique contribution to graphic design was to add the power of developing technologies to Weingart's pioneering style, specifically the Apple Macintosh computer.

Greiman had become the first designer to embrace computer technology and she used the newly launched Macintosh as a design tool (as opposed to a production tool), making use of pixellation and software error as positive elements. With the Macintosh came a new approach to design; unchartered boundaries,with a medium yet to have any rules set in place.

Weingart lectured regularly at Cranbrook Academy of Art, in Michigan, one of the first American educational institutions to be receptive to the New Wave. The interest originated from Katherine McCoy, the then co-chair of the graphic design department, whose belief in 'typography as discourse' (meaning that the viewing of an image and reading of text should be one action, not two separate practices) predisposed her to Weingart. Discussions often turned to the relationship between theory and design – mostly theories around deconstructionism and postmodernism. In fact, New Wave design is now practically synonymous with the concept of postmodernism.

Jamie Reid

Jamie Reid's name and reputation is inseparable from the British punk movement that emerged in the mid-1970s. Central to his work was the use of type that was presented in a crude, Dadaist, ransom-note style, the letters clearly having been cut from newspapers and magazines. His most iconic designs remain those that he produced for punk band the Sex Pistols, which demonstrated a remarkably astute graphic interpretation of the movement, at once provocative and shocking.

Born 1947, Croydon, England
Importance British artist and designer, considered to be the graphic voice of British punk

Reid took an art foundation course at Wimbledon Art School before continuing his studies at Croydon Art School. At the time he was inspired by the situationist movement in Paris, France, and in particular by their protests, sloganeering, graffiti and posters. Reid and fellow student Malcolm McLaren even staged a sit-in at Croydon in 1968, in solidarity with an identical protest that was taking place at the Sorbonne in Paris.

In 1970, Reid unleashed a visual language inspired by the situationists when he co-founded the *Suburban Press*, which in his own words was a 'very anarchist, situationist' radical political magazine. Producing the magazine, posters and leaflets

Reid's 1977 iconic design for the Sex Pistols' single God Save the Queen.

'agitprop' style on a tiny budget, in support of socio-political causes such as black rights and feminism, Reid became adept at cutting letters and photographs from newspapers to create arresting layouts. He described this as early experiments with a 'ripped and torn punk image'.

In 1974, Reid designed the first British language anthology of situationist writings, *Leaving the 20th Century*. The book's jacket featured the title scrawled in black marker pen over a white background – an aesthetic that has since influenced the entire do-it-yourself design language of fanzines.

Around the same time, Malcolm McLaren asked Reid to art-direct the image of a band he was managing, the Sex Pistols. Reid's iconic sleeve design for their first single, *Anarchy in the UK*, was a synthesis of all his work to date. The band's name and song title were presented as patches, clipped onto a trampled, burnt and torn Union Jack, covered in safety pins. Intended as an attack on the establishment, Reid won overnight infamy.

The same controversy greeted his sleeve design and accompanying poster for *God Save the Queen*, for which Reid manipulated a Cecil Beaton portrait of Queen Elizabeth II, placing the title of the song over her eyes and the band's name across her mouth. For the poster advertising the single, the same portrait was again manipulated, but this time the Queen's lips were pierced and held secure by a safety pin. The title and band's name (and even a lyric excerpt) were hand-written around the image on a white background.

Next came explicitly situationist-influenced designs for the sleeves of *Pretty Vacant* and *Holidays In the Sun*. The zenith of Reid's graphic interpretation of punk came with the sleeve design for the Sex Pistols' album, *Nevermind the Bollocks, Here's the Sex Pistols* – a bold colourful cover, using yellow, black and pink, laid over with ransom-letter type.

Reid's position in the graphic design canon continues to revolve around his iconic punk imagery, which communicated the visual language of punk in the most vivid, imaginative and aggressive terms.

SITUATIONISM
A radical left-wing political and cultural movement, which commenced with the founding of the Situationist International by various avant-garde artistic groups in 1957. Their activism and relevance peaked with the Paris uprisings in 1968.

Index

For main entries see contents page. References to graphic designers are only given when mentioned other than their main entry.